THE BEST
Pet Name Book

SECOND EDITION

Wayne Bryant Eldridge, DVM

Illustrations by Tom Kerr

EVER!

ANTONY & CLEOPATRA

BARRON'S

Excerpts from *Old Possum's Book of Practical Cats* by T. S. Eliot, copyright 1939 by T. S. Eliot and renewed 1967 by Esme Valerie Eliot, reprinted by permission of Harcourt Brace Jovanovich, Inc. and Faber and Faber Limited.

Excerpts from "How to Name a Dog" copyright © 1948 James Thurber. Copyright © 1975 Helen Thurber and Rosemary A. Thurber. From *The Beast in Me and Other Animals,* published by Harcourt Brace Jovanovich, Inc.

Excerpts adapted from *The Animals' Who's Who* by Ruthven Tremain. Reprinted with permission of Charles Scribner's Sons, an imprint of Macmillan Publishing Company, and Routledge & Kegan Paul Limited. Copyright © 1982 by Ruthven Tremain.

Peanuts cartoon by Charles Schultz, copyright United Features Syndicate. Reprinted with permission of U.S.F. Inc.

Excerpt from *The Will Rogers Book* by Paula Love, copyright 1972 by Texian Publishing Company. Reprint with permission.

About the Author

Dr. Wayne Bryant Eldridge is a veterinarian, as well as founder of Eldridge Animal Hospital, Pets First Veterinary Center and The Pet Place Veterinary Center in San Antonio, Texas, where he has practiced his profession for 25 years.

He earned his undergraduate degree and a Doctor of Veterinary Medicine from Texas A&M University in 1971.

Dr. Eldridge is an author and speaker on various topics pertaining to veterinary medicine and pets. His areas of special interest include animal behavior and the human-animal bond.

All inquiries should be addressed to:
Barron's Educational Series, Inc.
250 Wireless Boulevard
Hauppauge, New York 11788

Library of Congress Catalog Card No. 96-14305

International Standard Book No. 0-8120-9661-4

Library of Congress Cataloging-in-Publication Data
Eldridge, Wayne Bryant.
    The best pet name book ever / Wayne Bryant Eldridge ; illustrations by Tom Kerr. — 2nd ed.
      p.   cm.
    ISBN 0-8120-9661-4
    1. Pets—Names. I. Kerr, Tom. II. Title.
SF411.3E43   1996
929.9'7—dc20   96-14305
                                CIP

PRINTED IN THE UNITED STATES OF AMERICA

987654321

ACKNOWLEDGMENTS

My parents, Adelene and Jack Eldridge, are to be commended for their unconditional love, for their guidance throughout the years, and for providing me with the means for my education.

I am very grateful to my children, Lori Eldridge Giesen and Wayne Bryant Eldridge, Jr. for their faith in me and for their assistance with this book.

Don Reis, Michael Tuller and the staff at Barron's have worked diligently and competently to make this book a reality.

DEDICATION

This book is dedicated to all caring pet owners and to the celebration of the human-animal bond.

CONTENTS

And out of the ground the Lord God
formed every beast of the field,
and every fowl of the air;
and brought them unto Adam
to see what he would call them: and
whatsoever Adam called every living creature,
that was the name thereof.

And Adam gave names to all cattle,
and to the fowl of the air,
and to every beast of the fields.

GENESIS *2: 19–20*

INTRODUCTION

During my twenty-five years as a practicing veterinarian, many of the recently acquired pets brought to me for their first examinations have had no names, not because of apathy on the owner's part but because of the lack of a guide in the name selection process; thus, the owners of these pets usually ask for my suggestions. The thousands of requests that I have received originally prompted me to collect unusual pet names; later, I categorized my growing list of names according to general subject areas, such as historical names and names of foods. This method of categorization has helped hundreds of my clients choose names—not just any name, but a unique one—for their pets. Consequently, I have decided to organize my categories into a book so that I can assist a wider range of pet owners.

The Best Pet Name Book Ever is a creative guide for naming those special animals in our lives. Some of the names in this book are the actual names of my patients taken from the files of my animal hospital; others come from interviews with pet owners; and the remainder results from research into the various categories into which I have classified the names. This book seeks to give you an overview of examples of pet names (in particular, those for dogs and cats, but not exclusively), and by no means constitutes a complete list, for the possibilities are limitless.

You should use *The Best Pet Name Book Ever,* then, not as the comprehensive source on this subject, but rather as a tool to spark your imagination.

When choosing one of the names from this book or one of your own invention, you should keep in mind a couple of helpful hints. First, pick a name that your pet can easily recognize. Cats and dogs respond better to one and two syllable words: "Ezekiel" is a creative choice; however, your cat will respond more readily to the shortened "Ziggy" or "Zeke." Also, avoid giving your dog a name that sounds like one of the basic commands ("No," "Down," "Sit," "Stay," "Come," etc.). A dog named "Star" may have difficulty distinguishing her name from "Stay." Nevertheless, do not let these considerations restrict your creativity. If you are determined to name your cat "Dante Alighieri," do so, but plan on called him "Dan" or "Ali." You can still tell your friends about the famous person for whom the cat is named.

Note: If another name within the same chapter appears in the body of an entry, SMALL CAPITALS make reference to that name—for example:

Cyprus The island where APHRODITE was born.

"Pretty Boy"

CHAPTER 1

Appearance

What's in a name? That which we call a rose
By any other name would smell as sweet.

William Shakespeare
from *Romeo and Juliet*

The most obvious and simplest way to name a pet is by its appearance. This basis for choosing a name works especially well for a new pet whose personality and peculiarities have not yet revealed themselves to you; however, you must keep in mind that as a pet ages, its appearance may change and the name you originally chose for your animal may no longer apply. For example, "Fur Ball" is a cute name for a kitten but may not suit a fully grown tomcat. Still, such a situation where the name may be inappropriate rarely occurs, and basing your pet's name on its appearance can result in a fascinating and appropriate name.

Appearance

Adobe
Agate
Albino
Amber
Angus Bull
Ashes
Baby Bear
Baby Boy
Baby Doll
Baby Girl
Baby Kitty
Badger
Bandit
Bat Cat
Bear
Beige-ing
Big 'n
Big Boy
Big Foot
Big One
Big Red
Biscuit
Bits
Bitsie
Bitsy
Black

Black Ace
Black Cat
Black Jack
Blackberry
Blackie
Blacky
Blanca
Blanco
Blanquita
Blinker
Blondie
Blue
Bob Cat
Boots
Bootsie
Boxcar
Brandy
Bright Eyes
Brillo
Britches
Brown Spots
Brownie
Browny
Bruiser
Buffey
Buffie

Buffy
Bunny
Bushy
Butter Fingers
Button
Buttons
Cali
Calico
Calley
Caracal
Carbon
Carmel
Caspar
Chalk Paw
Charcoal
Charmin
Checkers
Chiquita
Chocolate
Chops
Chubbs
Chubby
Cinder
Cinnamon
Clay
Cobalt

Coco
Coco Bear
Cocoa
Cookie
Copper
Cotton
Cottonball
Cottontail
Coyote
Crackers
Cream
Crimson
Crystal
Cue Ball
Curlie
Curly
Curry
Cutey
Daffy
Darkie
Daylight
Diamond
Dinky
Dog
Doll
Domino

Droopy
Dust Mop
Dusty
Ebony
Eclipse
Eight Ball
Elkie
Ember
Fancy
Fang
Fat Boy
Fat Cat

Fatso
Fawn
Feather(s)
Flame
Flaps
Floppy
Flopsy
Fluffy
Four Paws
Foxie
Foxy Lady
Freckles

Frostie
Frosty
Fudge
Funny Face
Fuzz Ball
Fuzzy
Genius
Ghost
Ginger
Ginger Snap
Gold Cat
Goldie

Gray
Gray Bear
Gray Cat
Gray Spots
Hairy
Half Pint
Hershey
Hi-Ho Silver
Hobbles
Hog
Honey
Hulk

"Floppy"

Appearance

Husky	Many Paws	Pee Wee	Rusty
Inky	Mauve	Pepper	Sable
Iota	Midget	Perky	Sage
Ivory	Midnight	Phantom	Sandy
Jaguar	Minnie Paws	Pig	Satin
Jaguarundi	Miss Pretty	Piglet	Sausage Dog
Jumbo	Mitten(s)	Pink Kitty	Scottie
Kaffir	Momma Cat	Pinky	Scruffy
Kong	Momma Dog	Porker	Serval
Lefty	Moose	Porky	Shadow
Leo	Mother Cat	Pretty Boy	Sherman (tank)
Licorice	Mouse	Pretty Girl	Shinola
Lilly White	Mud	Pudgy	Shorty
Lion	Muffin	Puff	Sienna
Little	Munchkin	Puff Ball	Silky
Little One	Nugget	Puffy	Slick (a snake)
Lobo	Nutmeg	Pug	Slim
Locket	Ocelot	Puma	Slinky
Longfellow	Onyx	Pumpkin	Smidgen
(a dachshund)	Orange Kitty	Pygmy	Smokey
Lumpy	Oreo	Q Ball	Smudge
Lynx	Oso	Rags	Sneakers
Mama Cat	Panda	Rainbow	Snow
Mama Kitty	Panther	Raven	Snow Bear
Manly	Patches	Red	Snowball
Manx	Paws	Runt	Snowflake

Snowman	Stash (moustache)	Tip	Webster (a duck)
Snowshoes	Stretch	Tippy	Weenie Dog
Snowy	Stripe(s)	Tiptoe	Weiner Dog
Socks	Striper	Tomcat	Whale
Spade	Stripie	Toothpick	Whiskers
Sparkle(s)	Swirl	Toy	Whitey
Speckles	Tabby	Tramp	Whitie
Splotch	Tar Baby	Trinket	Wildcat
Spot(s)	Target	Twiggy	Wolf
Spotty	Tawny	Twinkles	Yellow
Squat	Ten	Ugly (Ug)	
Squint	Tiger	Velcro	
Squirt	Tiny	Velvet	

"*I think it all started when they decided to call me Happy Cat.*"

CHAPTER 2

Personality

Animals are such agreeable friends—they ask no questions, they pass no criticisms.

George Eliot (Mary Ann Cross)
from *Mr. Gilfil's Love Story*

Personality, like appearance, is one of the most obvious characteristics upon which to base a pet's name, but as I mentioned in Chapter 1, a new pet's personality may not fully emerge at first, and personality, like appearance, may change as a pet grows older. While it is important to remember these considerations when choosing your pet's name, a name derived from a dominant personality trait will usually prove appropriate throughout your pet's life.

Personality

Amble	Chancy	Digger	Fruity
Angel	Chaos	Ding-a-ling	Fury
Anxious	Charmer	Dingbat	Gabby
Apathy	Chase	Dingy	Genius
Attack	Chatterbox	Dirtball	Ginger Snapper
Audacious Lady	Chewie	Dodger	Goofus
Baby Bear	Chewy	Dr. Jekyll	Goofy
Baby Kitty	Chuckles	Dracula	Goony
Back Talk	Comet	Duster	Grabber
Bad Cat	Cool	Fearless	Gremlin
Badger	Couch Potato	Feisty	Groovy
Ballerina	Country	Fighter	Grumpy
Bandit	Coyote	Finesse	Gunner
Banshee	Cozy	Flake	Gypsy
Barky	Crash	Flakey	Happy
Bear	Crazy	Flash	Happy Cat
Blinky	Crunch	Flip	Hiccup
Blitz	Cuddles	Flounder	Hidey Cat
Blue	Cujo	Fox	Highball
Bomber	Cutter	Foxy	Hobo
Bonkers	Daffy	Fraidy Cat	Hokey
Bully	Dancer	Freeloader	Honey
Candy	Dandy	Friendly	Hoover
Caracal	Dash	Friskie	Hot Dog
Chainsaw	Demon	Frisky	Howler
Chance	Dennis the Menace	Front Porch Cat	Hugger

Hunter	Lovey	Nocturne	Rowdy
Ice	Lucky	Nosey	Rumble
Impulse	Lynx	Ocelot	Runner
Itchy	Magic	Oddball	Sassy
Jaguar	Mama Trouble	Ornery	Saucy
Jaguarundi	Manly	Pampas	Scamp
Jaws	Mate	Peppy	Scarlet
Jet	Meathead	Pistol	Schitzo
Jinx	Meow	Play Kitty	Scooter
Jumper	Mew	Pokey	Scout
Kaffir	Mew-Mew	Pompous	Scrapper
Killer	Mickey Mouth	Prancer	Scrappy
Kinky	Mischief	Prissy	Scratches
Lady	Miss Piggy	Puddles	Screwball
Lefty	Miss Priss	Puma	Serval
Leo	Miss Sassy	Punch	Shadow
Licker	Monkey	Pushy	Shady
Licky	Moody	Quick	Sharp
Lightnin'	Motor	Radar	Shock
Lion	Mouser	Rambler	Shocker
Loner	Moxy	Ranger	Shredder
Lonesome	Mr. Hyde	Rascal	Sir Lick-a-Lot
Looney	Nibbler	Rebel	Sissy
Lover	Nibbles	Roque	Skamp
Lover Boy	Nightmare	Rough	Skamper
Lover Girl	Noble	Rover	Skidatel

Personality

Sleazy
Sleek
Sleepy
Slipper
Slow Poke
Slumber
Sly
Smooch
Snapback
Snapper
Snappy
Sneaky
Sneezy
Sniffer
Sniffles
Sniffy
Snuggler
Snuggles
Solo

Spacey
Speedy
Spinner
Spirit
Splash
Spooky
Spunky
Squeaky
Squiggles
Steer
Sticker
Stinky
Stray
Stray Cat
Stupid
Swishie
Taffy
Tag
Teaser

Teddy Bear
Terminator
Thumper
Tiger
Tom
Tough Cat
Tracker
Tramp
Trip
Tripper
Trooper
Trotter
Troubles
Trusty
Tuffy
Tugger
Turbo
Vagrant
Valiant

Vampire
Vanity
Wags
Warrior
Watchcat
Watchdog
Weasel
Weedeater
Wiggles
Wild Thing
Wildcat
Winker
Winky
Woofer
Worm
Worthless

"Jacques" (and friend)

CHAPTER 3

Human Names

The Naming of Cats is a difficult matter,
. . . First of all, there's the name that the family uses daily,
Such as Victor or Jonathan, George or Bill Bailey—
All of them sensible everyday names.
There are fancier names if you think they sound sweeter,
Some for the gentlemen, some for the dames:
Such as Plato, Admetus, Electra, Demeter . . .

T. S. Eliot
from *Old Possum's Book of Practical Cats*

A pet with a human name tends to have a special relationship with its owner, who often regards the pet as a surrogate child or best friend. In fact, many owners name their pets after a person they have known, a relative, or someone they admire. Frequently, a human name can best depict the character, or nature, of a pet; for instance, "Reginald" vividly suggests the qualities of a basset hound. Likewise, a pet may resemble—hopefully not to a great extent—someone you know. If you can name your pet after this person without offending him or her, then you have further established your pet's unique identity.

Human Names

Aaron	Amos	Barnie	Bobby
Abby	Amy	Barry	Bonnie
Abe	Andre	Bart	Boris
Abigail	Andrea	Bartholomew	Bosley
Adam	Andy	Basil	Brad
Adelene	Angela	Bea	Bradley
Adolph	Ann	Beau	Brady
Adriana	Anna	Becky	Brando
Agatha	Anne	Belle	Brandon
Agnes	Annette	Ben	Brandy
Al	Annie	Benji	Brent
Alan	April	Bentley	Brett
Albert	Arby	Bernard	Brewster
Alec	Armstrong	Bernie	Brian
Alex	Arnie	Bert	Bridget
Alexander	Arnold	Bertha	Bridgette
Alfred	Arthur	Bessie	Britt
Alice	Ashleigh	Beth	Brittany
Alisa	Ashley	Betsy	Brooke
Alison	Audrey	Bianca	Brooks
Allan	Babette	Bill	Bruce
Allen	Bailey	Billie	Bruno
Allison	Barbie	Billy	Brutus
Amanda	Barkley	Billy Bob	Bryan
Amando	Barnaby	Blaire	Bryant
Amelia	Barney	Bobbi	Bubba

Bubba Smith	Celia	Cliff	Darcy
Buck	Charles	Clifford	Darren
Bud	Charley	Clint	David
Buddy	Charlie	Clinton	Davy
Burt	Charlotte	Cody	Dawn
Buford	Chaz	Colby	Debbie
Butch	Chelsea	Colette	Dee
Byron	Cher	Colleen	Dennis
Calvin	Cheryl	Colline	Derek
Cammie	Chester	Connie	Derrick
Cammy	Chet	Corey	Devan
Candice	Chris	Courtney	Dexter
Carley	Christina	Craig	Diana
Carlos	Christopher	Crystal	Dodie
Carmella	Chuck	Curt	Dody
Carmen	Ciel	Curtis	Dollie
Carol	Cindy	Cynthia	Dolly
Casey	Clancy	Daisy	Dominic
Casper	Clara	Dale	Dominique
Cassidy	Clare	Damon	Don
Cassie	Clark	Dan	Donald
Caterina	Claudia	Dana	Donna
Catherine	Clay	Daniella	Donnie
Cathy	Clem	Danielle	Dory
Catrina	Clementine	Danny	Dot
Cecil	Cleo	Daphne	Dottie

Human Names

Doug	Emma	Fred	Gretta
Douglas	Eric	Freddie	Guido
Drew	Erik	Freddy	Gunther
Dudley	Erin	Frederick	Gussie
Duncan	Ernest	Gabby	Gwen
Dustin	Ethan	Gary	Hailey
Dwayne	Eunice	Gayle	Haley
Dylan	Eva	Gene	Hans
Earl	Evan	George	Harold
Edgar	Evette	Georgette	Harry
Edie	Ezra	Georgia	Harv
Edward	Faith	Gerard	Harvey
Edwin	Fannie	Gerrie	Hattie
Edy	Fay	Gertie	Hazel
Elaine	Felicia	Gertrude	Heather
Eli	Felix	Gina	Helen
Elisabeth	Fergie	Ginger	Henry
Elizabeth	Fletch	Ginnie	Herbie
Ellen	Flo	Ginny	Herman
Ellie	Floyd	Gloria	Hilary
Elliot	Fran	Golda	Hilda
Elsa	Francine	Grace	Hogan
Elsie	Francis	Gracey	Hollis
Elvira	Frank	Gracie	Holly
Emilio	Frankie	Greg	Howard
Emily	Frannie	Gretchen	Huey

Ian	Jennie	John Henry	Kay
Igor	Jennifer	Johnny	Kelly
Ilsa	Jenny	Jonathan	Kent
Inga	Jeremy	Jones	Kerry
Ingrid	Jerry	Joni	Kevin
Ira	Jess	Jonie	Kim
Irving	Jesse	Jordan	Kimberly
Isa	Jessica	Joseph	Kimbrey
Ivan	Jessie	Josephine	Kit
Jack	Jezabel	Josh	Kristen
Jackie	Jill	Josie	Kristie
Jacob	Jim	Joya	Kristy
Jacques	Jimmie	Joyce	Lacey
Jake	Jimmy	Judy	Lacie
James	Joan	Jules	Lance
Jamie	Joann	Julia	Lanna
Jan	Joanne	Julie	Larry
Jane	Jock	Julius	Laura
Janie	Jodie	Justin	Lauren
Jason	Jody	Karen	Lea
Jasper	Joe	Kate	Leanne
Jean	Joel	Katherine	Lee
Jedgar	Joela	Kathryn	Leland
Jeffrey	Joey	Kathy	Lena
Jen	John	Katie	Leroy
Jenna	John Alex	Katy	Lesley

Human Names

Leslie	Luigi	Mathilda	Millie
Lester	Luke	Matt	Mindy
Lianna	Maddy	Matthew	Mira
Libby	Madeline	Mattie	Miriam
Lilli	Maggie	Maude	Missy
Lilly	Magnum	Maudie	Misty
Linda	Malcolm	Maureen	Mitch
Lindsay	Mandy	Maven	Molly
Lisa	Mangus	Mavis	Monique
Liz	Marcey	Max	Montgomery
Liza	Marcia	Maxine	Monty
Lizzy	Marcie	May	Morris
Lois	Marcus	Maynard	Muriel
Lola	Marge	McGee	Murphy
Lolita	Margie	Meagan	Murray
Lollie	Margo	Meg	Nadine
Lora	Maria	Megan	Nance
Loren	Marianne	Melissa	Nancy
Lori	Marie	Melvin	Naomi
Lottie	Mark	Mia	Natalie
Lou	Marlene	Michael	Nathan
Louie	Marsha	Michelle	Ned
Louis	Marshie	Mickey	Neil
Louise	Martha	Mike	Nell
Lucas	Martin	Mikey	Nellie
Lucy	Marvin	Miles	Nelly

Newt	Percival	Rhett	Samantha
Nicholas	Percy	Rick	Sandy
Nick	Pete	Ricky	Sara
Nicky	Petey	Riley	Sarah
Nicole	Petra	Rita	Saul
Niki	Petula	Robert	Schroder
Noel	Phil	Robin	Schultz
Nora	Philip	Roger	Scott
Norman	Phoebe	Ron	Scottie
Olin	Phyllis	Ronald	Sean
Olive	Polly	Ronney	Sebastian
Oliver	Pollyanna	Ronnie	Seth
Ollie	Priscilla	Roscoe	Seymour
Oscar	Prudy	Rose	Shannon
Otto	Rachel	Roxanne	Sharon
Pam	Ralph	Roy	Shawn
Pamela	Randolph	Rudy	Shayne
Panchito	Randy	Russell	Sheila
Pancho	Raquel	Rusty	Shelby
Parker	Raymond	Ruth	Shelly
Patrick	Reba	Ryan	Sherry
Patty	Rebecca	Sabre	Shirley
Paula	Reginald	Sabrina	Sibyl
Pearl	Rene	Sadie	Sid
Peg	Renee	Sally	Sidney
Penelope	Rex	Sam	Sophie

Human Names

Sophie	Tanya	Tracy	Walter
Stacey	Taylor	Travis	Warren
Stanley	Ted	Trenton	Wayne
Stella	Teddy	Trevor	Webster
Stephanie	Teena	Trish	Wendy
Stephen	Templeton	Trudy	Wilbur
Steven	Teresa	Tucker	William
Stuart	Teri	Tyler	Willie
Sue	Tessi	Valerie	Willy
Susan	Tessie	Van	Wilma
Susie	Theodore	Vanessa	Windy
Susy	Thomas	Vaughan	Winnie
Suzanne	Tiffany	Vera	Winston
Suzette	Timmy	Vic	Woodrow
Suzie	Timothy	Vick	Wylie
Suzy	Tina	Vicky	Yvette
Sylvia	Toby	Victor	Yvonne
Tabitha	Tom	Vigil	Zachary
Tamara	Tommy	Virginia	Zane
Tammy	Tony	Wally	Zeke

"Cleo"

"Honey Bunny"

CHAPTER 4

Terms of Endearment

I am driven to the conclusion that my sense of kinship with animals is greater than most people feel. It amuses me to talk to animals in a sort of jargon I have invented for them; and it seems to me that it amuses them to be talked to, and they respond to the tone of the conversation, though its intellectual content may to some extent escape them.

George Bernard Shaw
from *Killing for Sport*

Many people use terms of endearment to refer to members of their families. A large number of people also use such terms when addressing their pets. Names such as "Baby" and "Sweetie" may not have originally been a dog's or cat's name, but by repeated use, an owner may come to refer to his or her pet in that manner. Many owners, however, initially choose a term of endearment for a special pet's name, and often the owner will create this affectionate name from his or her own heart.

Terms of Endearment

Ace	Fifi	Kissy Bear	Punkin
Angel	Fluffer	Kissy Face	Purdy
Babe	Fu Fu	Kitter	Sugar
Baby	Fuffy	Lad	Sugar 'n Spice
Baby Bear	Gin Gin	Laddie	Sugar Baby
Baby Cakes	Ginger Sugar	Lov-a-Lot	Sugar Bear
Baby Doll	Gingi Girl	Lover Boy	Sugar Pie
Baby Girl	Girly	Lover Girl	Sugar Plum
Baby Kitty	Hey Girl	Lovey	Sugarfoot
Beau Beau	Honey	Lovey Lou	Sugarkins
Bitsie	Honey Blue	Lovums	Sunshine
Bitsy	Honey Bunny	Marshmallow	Sweet Pea
Bubby	Honey Dew	Nuffin	Sweet Thing
Buffer	Hot Dog	Patty Cake	Sweetie
Cutsie	Hotlips	Precious	Sweetie Pie
Dickens	Itsy-Bitsy	Pudden	Sweetums
Duster	Junior	Puddin'	Tootsie
Dusty	Keeper	Puddy Tat	True Blue

"Marshmallow"

"Washington"

CHAPTER 5

Historical Names

I never have been able to get very far in the exploration of the minds of people who call their dogs Mussolini, Tojo, and Adolf, and I suspect the reason is that I am unable to associate with them long enough to examine what goes on in their heads. I nod, and I tell them the time of day, if they ask, and that is all.

James Thurber
from *How to Name a Dog*

Many owners choose historical names for their pets, either because they enjoy history or because a particular historical figure interests them, and sometimes, a pet may actually resemble a well-known character from history. For instance, the name "Napoleon Bonaparte" would accurately describe a small feisty dog. This chapter contains the names of some famous—and some not-so-famous—dogs and cats of the past and a sampling of the names of the prominent figures of world history. The list of the latter is by no means complete; it only illustrates some of the names that other pet owners have used.

Historical Names

Agrippina	The mother of the Roman emperor NERO. He had her murdered.
Alexander	(1) The name of three of the Russian czars. (2) Alexander of Macedonia, conqueror of the ancient world, who was known as "Alexander the Great."
Ambrose (Saint)	A bishop of Milan in the fourth century A.D. who was one of the most influential men of his time.
Appleseed, Johnny	John Chapman (1774–1845). The orchards of the Midwest grew from the seed that this nurseryman was reported to have spread across the land.
Aristotle	One of the greatest Greek thinkers and philosophers (384–322 B.C.) whose writings have had a major influence on the world.
Attila	King of the Huns called the "Scourge of God" by peoples he conquered during the fifth century.
Aztec	The Aztecs were a group of people that originated in northwest Mexico, becoming a small nomadic tribe in the twelfth century, eventually expanding into a huge empire.
Bailey (James A.)	The British circus proprietor who merged with P. T. Barnum's traveling circus in 1881.
Balto	A black, long-haired malamute that in February, 1925 led Gunnar Kasson's dog team through a blizzard to reach diphtheria-plagued Nome, Alaska with antitoxin serum. A statue of Balto stands in New York City's Central Park.
Barnum (P. T.)	Phineas Taylor Barnum (1810–1891), co-founder of "The Barnum and Bailey Greatest Show on Earth."

Beau — General Omar BRADLEY'S pet poodle.

Beauregard — A Confederate general whose full name was Pierre Gustave Toutant de Beauregard.

Bessie — A collie that belonged to President Calvin Coolidge, the thirtieth President of the United States (1923–1929).

Big Ben — The fox terrier that belonged to President Herbert Hoover, named for the famous London clock.

Billy the Kid — William Bonney (1859–1881). A ruthless Wild West criminal who killed a man before reaching his teens.

Bingo — The black-and-white dog on Cracker Jack boxes.

Bismarck — Otto Eduard Leopold von Bismarck (1815–1898), a Prussian statesman who united the German states into one empire and created the Triple Alliance between Germany, Austria-Hungary and Italy, thus preserving peace in Europe until World War I.

Blackberry — One of President Calvin Coolidge's pet dogs.

Blackie — A mixed-breed dog that belonged to the author when he was a child.

Blacky — President Calvin Coolidge's black cat.

Blanco — A white collie that a little girl in Illinois gave to President Lyndon B. Johnson during his term in office.

Bluegrass — Daniel BOONE'S family cat.

Bonham — A hero of the Battle of the Alamo (1836).

Historical Names

Boone (Daniel) Hero of the early West who was a famous Indian fighter and frontiersman.

Bradley (Omar Nelson) An American general who commanded troops in Europe in World War II.

Brutus The Roman general and orator who led the plot to murder Julius Caesar in 44 B.C.

Buddy The female German shepherd who was the first Seeing Eye dog. Buddy belonged to Morris Frank, a blind man from Tennessee, and was trained in Switzerland at the kennels where Dorothy Harrison Eustis, the founder of The Seeing Eye Inc., worked. Frank told Buddy's story in his book, *First Lady of Seeing Eye*.

Buffalo Bill William Cody (1846–1917), was a famous hunter and scout who starred in and operated his own Wild West show.

Bush (George) The forty-first President of the United States.

Caesar (Julius) The Roman general and statesman who became dictator of Rome, ending the era of the Roman Republic.

Charlemagne The great military leader who became the first Holy Roman Emperor from A.D. 800–814.

Charlie One of President John F. Kennedy's dogs.

Checkers A black-and-white cocker spaniel sent to Richard Nixon when he was running for vice president. Nixon revealed Checkers' existence when he appeared on television on September 23, 1952, to combat allegations that he had received illegal campaign funds. His speech has since been called the Checkers Speech.

Chips	A shepherd-husky-collie mix that was the first member of the army's K-9 Corps sent overseas in World War II. Chips landed in Sicily in July 1943 and aided pinned-down American troops by attacking Italian gunners. He received decorations for this act and returned home in 1945.
Cicero	The statesman and orator who tried to save the dying Roman Republic.
Cleopatra	The name for the seven queens of ancient Egypt. The most famous was Cleopatra VII (69–30 B.C.), who was the subject of many literary works, including Shakespeare's *Antony and Cleopatra* and *Caesar and Cleopatra* by George Bernard Shaw.
Cloe	A dog that belonged to George WASHINGTON, first President of the United States (1789–1797).
Cochise	Chief of the central Chiricahua in Southeastern Arizona (1800–1874), the most famous Apache leader to resist intrusions by whites.
Constantine	Flavius Valerius Constantinus (A.D. 280–337); also known as Constantine the Great, the first Roman emperor to adopt Christianity.
Crockett (Davy)	Famous frontiersman who died at the Battle of the Alamo (1836).
Cuba	One of Ernest Hemingway's forty cats.
Custer (George Armstrong)	The famous American army officer who lost his life in a battle against the Indians at Little Bighorn, which has become known as Custer's Last Stand.
Durkheim (Emile)	The French sociologist and founder (1859–1917) of modern sociology as an academic discipline.

Historical Names

Einstein (Albert)	The German-American physicist (1879–1955) who published the Theory of Relativity in 1905.
Fala	The Scottish terrier that Franklin D. Roosevelt humorously defended against unjustified attacks by his political opponents.
Ferdinand	A king of Spain who, with his wife Isabella, received Christopher Columbus at the Court in Barcelona and agreed to finance his voyage.
Fido	The yellow mongrel belonging to Abraham Lincoln's two sons, Willie and Tad. Fido stayed behind in Springfield, Illinois when the President-elect and his family moved to Washington.
Freebo	One of six dogs owned by President Ronald Reagan during his presidency.
Freud (Sigmund)	The famous psychoanalyst (1856–1939) whose work profoundly affected the study and practice of psychology and psychiatry.
Galilei (Galileo)	Italian astronomer, mathematician, and physicist (1564–1642).
Gandhi (Mohandas Karamchand)	The great Indian statesman (1869–1948) who freed his country from British rule through nonviolent resistance. Gandhi is considered the father of modern India.
Genghis Khan	The great Mongol ruler (1167–1227) who conquered a vast empire, including China.
Geronimo	Apache Indian leader (1829–1909) who eventually became a rancher. While in St. Louis for the Louisiana Purchase Exposition, he rode in President Theodore Roosevelt's inaugural parade in 1905.
Golda Meir	The woman who became Prime Minister of Israel in 1969.

Gorbachev (Mikhail)	Soviet leader (b. 1931) from 1985 to 1991.
Grits	The dog belonging to President Jimmy Carter's daughter, Amy.
Handsome Dan	The white bulldog that was the original Yale bulldog mascot. The first Handsome Dan has been followed by a series of namesakes, one of which still represents Yale today.
Heidi	A Weimaraner owned by President Dwight D. Eisenhower.
Her	One of the pair of beagles that accompanied President Lyndon B. Johnson and his family to the White House. Johnson received much criticism when he lifted Her and the other beagle HIM up by the ears.
Him	The other half of President Lyndon B. Johnson's pair of beagles. (See HER)
Hitler (Adolf)	The totalitarian ruler of Germany's Third Reich who initiated World War II and was responsible for the slaughter of millions of people.
Houdini (Harry)	The famous magician (1874–1926) who could escape from any contraption devised to hold him.
Igloo	The troublesome fox terrier that traveled with Admiral Richard E. Byrd on his first trip to the Antarctic (1928–1930).
Ike	The nickname of Dwight David Eisenhower, the Supreme Commander of the Allied armies in Europe in World War II. Eisenhower later became President of the United States (1953–1961).
Isabella	Queen of Spain and wife of FERDINAND.

Historical Names

Ivan	The name of several Russian rulers. Ivan IV (1533–1584), known as "Ivan the Terrible," was the first Russian czar.
Jackson (Stonewall)	The Confederate general during the Civil War, second only to General Robert E. Lee.
James (Jesse)	The notorious bank and train robber who vandalized the American West during the nineteenth century.
Jo-Fi	Psychoanalyst Sigmund Freud's beloved chow.
King Timahoe	The Irish setter owned by President Richard Nixon.
King Tut	President Herbert Hoover's pet German shepherd dog.
Kublai Khan	Mongol emperor (c. 1216–1294), who was the grandson of Genghis Khan.
Laddie Boy	The Airedale that belonged to President Warren G. Harding.
Lady	One of George WASHINGTON'S pet dogs.
Laika	The female Samoyed that was the first living creature to orbit the earth in the second Soviet Sputnik.
Liberty	President Gerald Ford's golden retriever.
Livingstone (David)	A famous British explorer who pioneered large parts of Africa during the nineteenth century.
Lucky	A black sheepdog owned by President Ronald Reagan. Of the six of President Reagan's dogs, only two resided at the White House—Lucky and REX.

Magellan (Ferdinand)	The Portuguese navigator who was the first person to sail around the world.
Major	A German shepherd that belonged to Franklin Delano Roosevelt.
Mao Tse-tung (Zedong)	One of the founders of the Chinese Communist Party in 1921 and the People's Republic of China in 1949.
Marco	A Pomeranian that belonged to Queen Victoria of England.
Marco Polo	A Venetian who was one of the first Europeans to travel in Asia during the late thirteenth century.
Marjorie	A diabetic black-and-white mongrel that was the first creature to be kept alive by insulin.
Maximilian	The Austrian whom the French installed as emperor of the short-lived Mexican throne (1864–1867).
Meggy	One of Franklin D. Roosevelt's pet dogs. FALA was Meggy's sire.
Merlin	The wizard and counselor of King Arthur from *The Tales of King Arthur and his Court*.
Micetto	Pope Leo XII's large black-striped cat. After the Pope's death, the cat went to live with the French ambassador to Rome, the Vicomte de Chateaubriand.
Millie	A mixed breed dog (part Irish setter, part collie) owned by President Ronald Reagan.

Historical Names

Millie	The English springer spaniel belonging to President and Mrs. George Bush. Mrs. Bush wrote a book about Millie.
Ming	The dynasty that ruled China from 1368 to 1644. The Ming period was one of artistic growth.
Montgomery (Bernard Law)	The British general who won fame during the African campaign and the invasion of Europe in World War II.
Mopsey	One of George WASHINGTON'S favorite dogs.
Moshe Dayan	A leading Israeli general and statesman (1915–1981).
Mushka	A dog that was placed in orbit by the Russians in one of the first Sputnik space vehicles.
Napoleon (Bonaparte)	The French general and military genius (1769–1821) who crowned himself Emperor of France and conquered much of Europe.
Neff (Pat)	A governor of Texas during the first half of the twentieth century and a president of Baylor University in Waco, Texas.
Nelson	A black cat, the favorite of Sir Winston Churchill, Prime Minister of Great Britain during most of World War II.
Nelson (Horatio)	Great Britain's greatest admiral and naval hero, who established Britain's rule of the seas in the 1800s.
Nero	One of the cruelest Roman emperors, who killed thousands of Christians.
Newton (Sir Isaac)	The English scientist, astronomer, and mathematician (1642–1727) who invented calculus and first established the laws of gravity.

Niña, Pinta, and Santa Maria	The three ships in Christopher Columbus's fleet when he discovered America on October 12, 1492.
Nipper	The fox terrier that appears with a phonograph in the RCA trademark.
Patton (George Smith)	An American general (1885–1945) who led the 3rd Army in Europe during World War II.
Pavlov (Ivan Petrovich)	The Russian physiologist who won the 1904 Nobel Prize in physiology and medicine for his research on conditioned reflexes.
Perruque	One of fourteen cats owned by Cardinal Richelieu when he died in 1642.
Plato	A famous Greek philosopher (c.428–c.348 B.C.) who was a follower of Socrates.
Pompey the Great	Roman general and statesman (106–48 B.C.) who was one of Julius Caesar's greatest adversaries.
Pompidou (Georges)	Premier and President (1911–1974) of France's Fifth Republic from 1962–1974.
Pushinka	A puppy from STRELKA'S litter that the Soviet Premier Nikita Khrushchev presented to Mrs. John F. Kennedy when she was First Lady.
Rasputin	The religious man (1865–1916) who corrupted Russia's Czar Nicholas II and his wife Alexandra.
Reagan (Ronald)	The motion picture actor and California governor who became the fortieth President of the United States.
Rex	A spaniel that belonged to President Ronald Reagan.

Historical Names

Ripley
(Robert Leroy)

An American cartoonist who began collecting strange and unusual facts that he eventually compiled into two *Believe It or Not* books.

Rob Roy

President Calvin Coolidge's white collie.

Rommel (Erwin)

The brilliant German general (1891–1944) who commanded the Afrika Korps and the forces defending Normandy in World War II.

Ross (Betsy)

Creator of the first U.S. flag.

Rover

The collie that was President Lyndon Johnson's first dog.

Rufus

A poodle owned by British Prime Minister Winston Churchill.

Sailor Boy

Theodore Roosevelt's pet dog.

Scannon

Meriwether Lewis's black Newfoundland that accompanied the Lewis and Clark expedition to the Pacific.

Searcher

One of George WASHINGTON's pet dogs.

Shannon

A dog that was the White House pet of John F. Kennedy, Jr.

Shasta

The first U.S.-born *liger,* the offspring of a male lion and a female tiger, to reach maturity. Shasta was born May 6, 1948, at the Hogle Zoological Garden in Salt Lake City, Utah.

Sherman
(William Tecumseh)

The famous Union general during the American Civil War.

Sizi

The cat that was a companion to Albert Schweitzer (1875–1965) when he was a medical missionary in Africa.

Skip	A mongrel dog owned by President Theodore Roosevelt.
Socrates	A noted Greek philosopher (470–399 B.C.) whose beliefs included justice and good moral character.
Stanley (Henry)	The British explorer who led the expedition to find David LIVINGSTONE.
Strelka	One of the two female Samoyed that the Soviet Union launched in Sputnik V on August 19, 1960.
Taca	A Siberian husky owned by President Ronald Reagan.
Thatcher (Margaret)	The former Prime Minister of Great Britain who was known as the "Iron Lady."
Tito	The Communist ruler of Yugoslavia after World War II. Tito declared Yugoslavia's independence from Soviet control.
Trafalgar	The cape on Spain's southern coast at the western entrance to the Strait of Gibraltar that was the sight of one of history's greatest naval battles: Great Britain, led by Admiral Horatio Nelson, defeated the combined French and Spanish fleets on October 21, 1805.
Traveler	The horse of Robert E. Lee, the Confederate general during the American Civil War.
Trojan	An inhabitant of Troy, an ancient city in Asia Minor that Homer made famous.
Uncle Sam	The personification of the United States; his top hat and red, white, and blue clothes make him a distinctive figure.

Victory	A golden retriever owned by President Ronald Reagan.
Viking	A member of the Scandinavian bands of sea rovers who raided England, Ireland, France, Germany, Italy, and Spain between the 700s and 1100s. The Vikings also settled Greenland and Iceland.
Washington (George)	Commander of the American forces during the Revolutionary War and first President of the United States.
Watson	(1) Alexander Graham Bell's assistant. (2) Sherlock Holmes' friend and assistant in the Arthur Conan Doyle fictional mysteries.
Winston (Churchill)	The Prime Minister of Great Britain from 1940 to 1945 and from 1951 to 1955, who was one of world history's greatest statesmen.
Wright (Orville and Wilbur)	Credited with flying the first airplane at Kitty Hawk, North Carolina, December 17, 1903.
Yuki	The small white dog adopted by President Lyndon B. Johnson in November 1966. Yuki quickly became the President's favorite dog.

"Winston"

ATHENA

CHAPTER 6

Greek and Roman Mythology

Far from Italy, far from my native Tarentum I lie;
And this is the worst of it—worse than death.
An exile's life is no life. But the Muses loved me.
For my suffering they gave me a honeyed gift:
My name survives me. Thanks to the Sweet Muses.
Leonidas will echo through all time.

Leonidas of Tarentum
from *The Greek Anthology*

The gods, goddesses, and other figures of mythology are known for both their colorful appearance and their vibrant personalities; furthermore, they generally have unusual, and therefore, memorable names. Thus, pets often are namesakes of these characters, and a pet's mythological name can provide a great source of conversation.

Achelous	A River God who turned himself into a bull to fight Heracles (see HERCULES) because the two men were both in love with the same woman, Deianira.
Achilles	The champion of the Greeks in the Trojan War.
Actaeon	A young hunter whom ARTEMIS turned into a stag because he had accidentally seen her naked. In his new form, Actaeon's own dogs chased and killed him.
Adonis	APHRODITE'S love, who spent half the year with her and the other half in the Underworld. A boar killed him, and a crimson flower sprung up where each drop of his blood fell.
Aeneas	The son of APHRODITE (Venus) who fought for TROY in the Trojan War. After the defeat he escaped to Italy where he founded the Roman race.
Aero	ORION'S love and the daughter of the King of Chios.
Aidos	The personified emotion of reverence and shame, which was esteemed highest of all feelings.
Ajax	One of the Greek champions in the Trojan War.
Alce	One of ACTAEON'S hounds; the name means "strength."
Alexander	Another name for PARIS, who caused the Trojan War and died of a wound from a poisoned arrow.
Althea	The mother of Meleager; she killed him and then killed herself.
Amarynthos	One of ACTAEON'S hounds.

Amazon	A member of the nation of women warriors who had no dealings with men except to oppose them in war and to breed children.
Andromache	The devoted wife of HECTOR, prince of TROY.
Andromeda	The daughter of CASSIOPEIA, who was punished for her mother's vanity. PERSEUS saved her from her fate, and she married him.
Antigone	The daughter of OEDIPUS. She was killed by CREON, his successor on the throne.
Aphrodite	The Goddess of Love and Beauty.
Apollo	The God of Light and Truth.
Arcas	The son of CALLISTO and ZEUS whom Zeus placed among the stars as Ursa Minor (Lesser Bear).
Ares	The God of War (Roman: Mars). The Son of ZEUS and HERA; he was a bully and also a coward, detested by his parents as well as others.
Argonauts	JASON and his followers who went on a quest to bring back the golden fleece. Their ship was the Argo.
Argos	ODYSSEUS'S dog. After being away at the Trojan War for twenty years, Odysseus returned to his home disguised as a beggar, and only Argos recognized him. The dog, too sick and weak to walk, wagged his tail in recognition; however, afraid of revealing his identity, Odysseus didn't acknowledge Argos, and as Odysseus walked on, Argos died.
Argus	HERA'S watchman with a hundred eyes.

Ariadne	King MINOS'S daughter who was deserted on the island of NAXOS by her lover, THESEUS.
Arion	The first horse, an offspring of POSEIDON.
Arne	Regarded as the ancestress of the Boeotian Greeks.
Artemis	The Goddess of Hunting and Wild Things.
Asbolos	One of ACTAEON'S hounds; the name means "soot-color."
Asopus	A River God.
Astraea	The daughter of ZEUS and THEMIS. She lived on earth happily during the Golden Age, but fled during the Bronze Age.
Atalanta	The maiden who could outshoot, outrun, and outwrestle most men. She eventually was turned into a lioness.
Ate	The Goddess of Mischief. Although a daughter of ZEUS, she was cast out of OLYMPUS.
Athena	The Goddess of the City, Protector of Civilized Life, Handicrafts, and Agriculture.
Atlas	The TITAN who held the world on his shoulders.
Attica	The country around Athens.
Aurora	The Goddess of Dawn.
Bacchus	Roman name for DIONYSUS, the God of the Vine.

Banos

One of ACTAEON'S hounds.

Battus

A peasant who saw HERMES steal APOLLO'S cattle. Hermes turned Battus into stone because the man broke his promise not to reveal the identity of the thief to Apollo.

Baucis

A poor old woman who was blessed by the gods, given a temple to live in, and promised that she would never live alone without her husband.

Bellona

The Roman name for ENYO, the Goddess of War.

Belus

The grandfather of the Danaïds (who were condemned to carry water in jars that were forever leaking.)

Biton

One of the two sons of Cydippe, a priestess of HERA. He and his brother yoked themselves to a wagon to carry their mother to pray. The journey killed both sons.

Boötes

The constellation just behind the Dipper. See ICARIUS.

Boreas

(1) The God of the North Wind who kidnapped and ravished Orithyia.
(2) One of ACTAEON'S hounds.

Bromius

Another name for DIONYSUS, who was a son of ZEUS. (See BACCHUS.)

Brontes

One of three CYCLOPS, each of whom had only one eye in the middle of his forehead.

Cabeiri

Dwarfs with supernatural powers. They protected the fields of Lemnos.

Cacus

The giant who stole cattle from Heracles' (HERCULES') flock.

Calliope	The daughter of ZEUS who was the MUSE of Epic Poetry.
Callisto	LYCAON'S daughter who was seduced by ZEUS and bore him a son, ARCAS. In a jealous rage, HERA turned Callisto into a bear, and when Arcas grew up placed his mother before him so that he would kill her. Zeus, however, saved Callisto and put her up in the stars as Ursa Major (Great Bear), placing Arcas beside her as Ursa Minor (Lesser Bear).
Calpe	The ancient Greek name for the Rock of Gibraltar.
Calypso	A nymph who kept ODYSSEUS prisoner on her island.
Camilla	A very skilled maiden warrior who was followed by a band of warriors.
Canache	One of ACTAEON'S hounds; the name means "ringwood."
Cassandra	One of PRIAM'S daughters. She became a prophetess because APOLLO loved her and gave her power of prognostication. Unfortunately, her prophecies were never believed.
Cassiopeia	ANDROMEDA'S mother, the Ethiopian queen, who was silly and vain and bragged that Andromeda was prettier than the daughters of the Sea God NEREUS.
Castor	The brother of POLLUX and the son of LEDA. He and his brother were the Protectors of Sailors.
Centaur	A creature who was half man and half horse.
Cerberus	The huge, fearsome watchdog of HADES. Cerberus guarded the gates of Hades, preventing spirits from leaving.

Ceres	The Roman name for DEMETER.
Chaos	The Nothingness that existed before the gods and before Creation.
Charites	Another name for the Graces who attended APHRODITE.
Charon	The boatman who guided the ferry that carried the dead souls to the gates of HADES.
Chediatros	One of ACTAEON'S hounds.
Circe	A beautiful and dangerous witch who turned men into beasts.
Cisseta	One of ACTAEON'S hounds.
Cleobis	BITON'S brother, son of Cydippe, a priestess of HERA. Cleobis perished with his brother after they yoked themselves to a wagon carrying their mother to pray.
Clio	The MUSE of History.
Clytie	A maiden who loved the Sun God, but whose love was not returned. She stared at him with longing until she turned into a sunflower.
Cora	Another name for PERSEPHONE.
Coran	One of ACTAEON'S hounds; the name means "crop-eared."
Cornucopia	The Horn of Plenty. Named after the horn of the goat, it was always full of food and drink.

Coronis	A maiden whom APOLLO loved, but who did not love him. She was unfaithful, so he killed her.
Cottus	A monster with a hundred hands.
Creon	The brother of JOCASTA. Creon became regent after OEDIPUS resigned the throne.
Cronus	A titan who was the father of ZEUS.
Cupid	Latin for EROS, the Greek God of Love.
Cyclops	A giant with only one eye in the middle of his forehead.
Cyllo	One of ACTAEON'S hounds; the name means "halt."
Cyllopotes	One of ACTAEON'S hounds; the name means "zigzagger."
Cynthia	Another name for ARTEMIS.
Cyprian	Another name for APHRODITE.
Cyprios	One of ACTAEON'S hounds.
Cyprus	The island where APHRODITE was born.
Dactyls	The women of Mount Ida, who were the first to make implements of iron.
Daphne	A huntress whose father, the River God Peneus, changed her into a tree to protect her from APOLLO who loved her.
Delian	Another name for APOLLO.

Delos	The island where APOLLO was born and where his temple stood.
Delphi	The site of APOLLO'S oracles.
Demeter	The Goddess of Corn. Sister of ZEUS, she bore him a daughter, PERSEPHONE.
Diana	The Roman name for ARTEMIS.
Dido	The founder and queen of Carthage. She threw herself on a pyre when AENEAS, whom she loved, left to search for a homeland in Italy.
Diomedes	A great Greek warrior at TROY.
Dione	A minor goddess. By some accounts, Dione and Zeus were APHRODITE'S parents.
Dionysus	The God of the Vine.
Dirce	The wife of LYCUS, the ruler of THEBES. Her grandsons and daughter killed her by tying her hair to a bull.
Dodona	ZEUS'S oracle, the oldest in Greece.
Dorian	A member of one of the prinicpal groups of ancient Greeks.
Doris	One of the 3,000 daughters of Ocean and wife NEREUS.
Draco	One of ACTAEON'S hounds; the name means "the dragon."
Dromas	One of ACTAEON'S hounds; the name means "the courser."

Dromios   One of ACTAEON'S hounds; the name means "seize 'em."

Dryad   One of the nymphs of the trees.

Echnobas   One of ACTAEON'S hounds.

Echo   The fairest of the nymphs who loved NARCISSUS; HERA condemned her never to talk unless she repeated what someone else had already said.

Electra   The daughter of Agamemnon and Clytemnestra. She avenged her father's murder by inciting her brother, ORESTES, to kill their mother and her lover.

Enyo   The Goddess of War.

Ephialtes   A giant. He and his twin brother wanted to prove themselves superior to the gods. For their presumption ARTEMIS killed them by making them accidentally slay each other.

Erato   The MUSE of Love Poetry.

Erigone   The daughter of ICARIUS, who hanged herself after finding her father murdered. DIONYSUS placed her in the heavens as Virgo.

Eris   The sister of ARES whose name means "discord."

Eros   The God of Love.

Eudromos   One of ACTAEON'S hounds; the name means "good runner."

Europa   A maiden with whom ZEUS fell in love. As a bull, he carried her off to Crete. The continent of Europe was named for her.

Eurus	The God of the East Wind.
Eurydice	The bride of ORPHEUS. She was killed by a viper sting after the wedding.
Fauna	The Roman Goddess of Fertility, sometimes called the Good Goddess.
Favonius	The Latin name for the West Wind.
Flora	The Roman Flower Goddess.
Galatea	(1) A sea nymph whom Polyphemus, the cyclops, loved. (2) The name of PYGMALION'S statue, which came to life.
Gemini	The constellation of the twin brothers, CASTOR and POLLUX.
Golden Fleece	The fleece of a ram that rescued PHRIXUS. He sacrificed it to ZEUS in thanksgiving. JASON subsequently led the quest for the Golden Fleece.
Gorgon	Dragonlike creatures with wings and snakes for hair, whose look turned men to stone.
Griffins	ZEUS'S hounds, which had the bodies of lions and the heads and wings of eagles. These beasts guarded the Gold of the North.
Hades	The God of the Underworld. He was the son of CRONUS and RHEA. (Hades is also used as a name for the Underworld itself.)
Harmonia	Cadmus's wife, who was the daughter of ARES and APHRODITE.
Harpale	One of ACTAEON'S hounds; the name means "voracious."
Harpeia	One of ACTAEON'S hounds; the name means "tear 'em."

Harpies	Flying creatures with hooked beaks and claws that left behind them a terrible stench that sickened all living creatures.
Hebe	The Goddess of Youth. She was the daughter of ZEUS and HERA.
Hecate	A triple deity who was Goddess of the Moon, Goddess of the Earth, and Goddess of the Underworld.
Hector	The brave, noble son of King PRIAM of TROY. Hector was the Trojan champion in the Trojan War.
Hecuba	The queen of TROY and wife of King PRIAM.
Helen	The daughter of ZEUS and LEDA, who was the fairest woman in the world. She married MENELAUS, but PARIS kidnapped her, starting the Trojan War.
Helicon	One of the MUSES' mountains. It was sacred to APOLLO whose temple was there.
Helios	The Sun God.
Hephaestus	The God of Fire.
Hera	ZEUS'S wife and sister. She was the Protector of Marriage and Married Women.
Heracles	See HERCULES.
Hercules	The Roman name for HERACLES, Greece's greatest hero and the strongest man alive.
Hermes	ZEUS'S messenger. He was sometimes called the "Master Thief."

Hermione	Unaware she had been promised to Orestes, MENELAUS gave her to ACHILLES' son, Pyrrhus.
Hero	The ill-fated lover of LEANDER. He died, and she killed herself.
Herse	An Athenian princess who was beloved by Hermes.
Hesper	The Goddess of the Evening Star.
Hesperides	The daughter of ATLAS, who with LADON (2), guarded the trees with golden branches, golden leaves, and golden apples.
Hestia	The Goddess of the Hearth.
Hilara	The daughter of APOLLO. Her name means "laughter-loving."
Himeros	The God of Desire who attended EROS. Also called Longing.
Hippodamia	Wife of PELOPS. He won her in a chariot race.
Hippolytus	The son of THESEUS whose second wife, PHAEDRA, fell in love with Hippolytus.
Hyacinth	A companion of APOLLO. He was accidentally killed when Apollo's discus hit him in the head. On each spot where a drop of his blood fell, a Hyacinth flower arose.
Hyades	Some nymphs whom ZEUS placed as the stars that bring rain when they are near the horizon.
Hydra	A nine-headed creature killed by HERACLES. (See HERCULES.)

Hypnos	The God of Sleep.
Iacchus	Another name for DIONYSUS. (See BACCHUS.)
Ibycus	A poet who lived around 550 B.C. When robbers left him mortally wounded he asked the cranes that were flying overhead to avenge him, and they did.
Icarus	The son of Daedalus, the architect. When Icarus flew too near the sun, the wax that held his wings in place melted. Icarus fell to earth and was killed.
Icarius	An Athenian, in Greek mythology, whom DIONYSUS taught how to make wine. Drunken shepherds murdered Icarius and threw him down a well, where his faithful dog, MAERA, found him. Dionysus honored Icarius, placing him among the stars as the constellation BOÖTES.
Icelus	The son of HYPNOS, who had the power to change himself into all sorts of birds and animals.
Ichnobate	One of ACTAEON'S hounds; the name means "tracker."
Ida	A nymph who took care of ZEUS when he was being hidden from Cronus.
Inachus	The father of IO.
Ino	The Sea Goddess who saved ODYSSEUS from drowning.
Io	The maiden who had an affair with ZEUS. He turned her into a white heifer to protect her from HERA'S jealous wrath. Unfortunately, Io, wound up in Hera's possession and spent years trying to escape and return to her original form. Finally, Zeus restored Io's humanity, and she spent the rest of her days happily.

Iphicles	Heracles' (HERCULES) half brother.
Iris	The Goddess of the Rainbow.
Ixion	The first murderer. Ixion also attempted to seduce HERA. ZEUS sentenced him to eternal punishment in HADES, where he was tied to a wheel and lashed with serpents.
Janus	A NUMINA who became personified. Janus was the God of Good Beginnings.
Jason	The leader of the quest for the GOLDEN FLEECE.
Jocasta	OEDIPUS'S mother and wife.
Jove	Another name for ZEUS.
Juna	The Roman name for HERA.
Jupiter	The Roman name for ZEUS.
Juturna	The Roman Goddess of Springs.
Kora	Another name for PERSEPHONE.
Labros	One of ACTAEON'S hounds; the name means "furious."
Lacena	One of ACTAEON'S hounds; the name means "lioness."
Lachne	One of ACTAEON'S hounds; the name means "glossy."
Lacon	One of ACTAEON'S hounds.

Ladon	(1) One of ACTAEON'S hounds. (2) The serpent who guarded the Golden Apples of the HESPERIDES.
Laertes	ODYSSEUS'S father.
Laius	The father of OEDIPUS. Oedipus unwittingly murdered him.
Lampos	One of ACTAEON'S hounds; the name means "shining one."
Lar	A NUMINA, who was the spirit of an ancestor. Every Roman family had a Lar.
Larvae	The spirits of HADES'S wicked dead, who were greatly feared.
Latinus	The great-grandson of SATURN and the king of the city of LATIUM.
Latium	A city in Italy that was conquered by AENEAS.
Latona	Another name for LETO.
Lavinia	The daughter of LATINUS and the wife of AENEAS. Together, husband and wife founded the Roman race.
Leander	HERO'S lover who killed herself after he drowned swimming to a rendezvous with her.
Leda	The wife of King Tyndareus of Sparta. ZEUS, in the form of a swan, seduced her.
Lelaps	(1) One of ACTAEON'S hounds; the name means "hurricane." (2) The hound destined to chase a fox until ZEUS finally changed them both to stone.

Lemures	Another name for LARVAE.
Lethe	The River of Forgetfulness in the Underworld.
Leto	Daughter of TITANS; APOLLO and ARTEMIS were her children by ZEUS.
Leucos	One of ACTAEON'S hounds; the name means "gray."
Liber	Another name for BACCHUS. (See DIONYSUS.)
Libera	A Roman name for PERSEPHONE. She was abducted by PLUTO, who wanted her to be queen of the Underworld.
Libitina	The Roman Goddess of the Dead.
Linus	The son of APOLLO and Psamathe. When his mother deserted him, dogs tore him apart.
Lityerses	A farmer who made strangers at his house reap. If they did less than he did, he cut off their heads, put their bodies in a sheaf, and sang a song. Heracles (HERCULES) killed him.
Lotis	A nymph who was changed into a lotus tree.
Lucina	Sometimes regarded as the Roman Goddess of Childbirth.
Luna	Latin for the Goddess of the Moon. The name Luna referred to DIANA.
Lyaeus	Another name for BACCHUS. (See DIONYSUS.)
Lycaon	A king of ATTICA and the father of CALLISTO. When he served human flesh at a banquet, ZEUS turned him into a wolf.

Lycisca	One of ACTAEON'S hounds.
Lycus	Ruler of THEBES and the husband of DIRCE. His daughter killed him because of his cruelty.
Lyncea	One of ACTAEON'S hounds.
Machaon	The Greeks' physician during the Trojan War.
Machimos	One of ACTAEON'S hounds; the name means "boxer."
Maeander	River in Phrygia that frequently changes its course.
Maera	A faithful dog, whose master ICARIUS was murdered and thrown into a well. Maera led Icarius's daughter ERIGONE to the body. She hanged herself and the dog then jumped into the well.
Maia	VULCAN'S wife. (See HEPHATETUS.)
Manes	The spirits of the good dead in HADES.
Marpessa	A maiden who chose the mortal Idas over APOLLO.
Mars	Roman name for ARES.
Medea	The daughter of King Colchias. A sorceress, she fell in love with JASON and helped him on his quest for the GOLDEN FLEECE.
Medusa	One of the GORGONS. PERSEUS cut off her head.
Megara	The wife of Heracles (HERCULES) and mother of three of his sons. Hercules went mad and killed them all.

Melampus	A great soothsayer whose pet snakes taught him animal language.
Melanchete	One of ACTAEON'S hounds; the name means "black-coated."
Melanea	One of ACTAEON'S hounds; the name means "black."
Melanion	The runner who beat ATALANTA and won her love.
Melicertes	The son of INO. After Ino and Melicertes jumped into the sea, to escape Athamas's wrath, Melicertes became a Sea God.
Melpomene	The MUSE of Tragedy.
Menelaus	The brother of Agamemnon and husband of HELEN.
Menelea	One of ACTAEON'S hounds.
Mentor	ODYSSSUS'S most trusted friend. ATHENA disguised herself as Mentor when she appeared to TELEMACHUS.
Mercury	The Roman name for HERMES.
Metis	ZEUS'S first wife, also called Prudence. Zeus swallowed her and developed a monumental headache, which eased only after ATHENA sprang from his head.
Midas	A king of Phrygia whose wish that everything he touched would turn to gold was granted.
Minerva	The Roman name for ATHENA.
Minos	One of the three judges in the Underworld.

Minotaur	A monster that was half bull and half human.
Minyas	The king of THESSALY. The ARGONAUTS, sometimes called the Minyae, were his descendants.
Moira	Fate, a mysterious power stronger than the gods. One who scorned Moira would meet NEMESIS.
Molossos	One of ACTAEON'S hounds.
Moly	An herb with white blossoms that HERMES gave ODYSSEUS to protect him from CIRCE'S spells.
Mopsus	Soothsayer of the ARGONAUTS, he also went on the Calydonian boar hunt.
Morpheus	The God of Sleep; also called the God of Dreams.
Mors	The God of Death; also called Thanatos.
Muse	One of nine daughters of ZEUS and Mnemosyne. They were goddesses of memory and then of the arts and sciences.
Myrmidon	One of a group of soldiers who fought against the TROJANS.
Napa	One of ACTAEON'S hounds; the name means "sired by a wolf."
Narcissus	A beautiful boy who scorned love despite many admiring ladies. Finally, he was cursed, fell in love with himself, and pined away for his own reflection in a pond.
Naxos	The island where THESEUS left ARIADNE.

Nebrophonos	One of ACTAEON'S hounds; the name means "fawn-killer."
Neleus	One of the twin sons of TYRO and POSEIDON.
Nemean Lion, The	The ferocious lion that ravaged the valley of Nemea, until Heracles (HERCULES) strangled the beast to death.
Nemesis	The Goddess of Righteous Anger, the personified emotion esteemed highest of all feelings.
Neptune	The Roman name for POSEIDON.
Nereid	A nymph of the sea and the daughter of NEREUS.
Nereus	The Old Man of the Sea. He had the power of prophecy and could assume any form he desired.
Nessus	A centaur who gave Heracles' (HERCULES') wife, Deianira, his blood as a love potion when he was dying.
Nestor	The wisest and oldest of the Greek chieftans.
Nike	The Greek Goddess of Victory.
Notus	The God of the South Wind.
Numina	The powers that were the Roman gods before the Romans adopted the Greek ones.
Ocydroma	One of ACTAEON'S hounds; the name means "swift runner."
Ocyrrhoe	A prophetess.

Odysseus	The Greek hero of the Trojan War, known for his cunning.
Oedipus	The king who was fated to kill his father and marry his mother.
Olympus	A mountain peak in Greece and home of the gods.
Ophion	A great serpent that ruled the TITANS before CRONUS.
Ops	The wife of SATURN (see CRONUS), who was the Goddess of the Harvest.
Orcus	The Roman name for the King of the Dead. (See HADES, PLUTO.)
Oresitrophos	One of ACTAEON'S hounds; the name means "mountain-bred."
Orestes	The son of Agamemnon and Clytemnestra. He avenged his father's murder by killing his mother and her lover.
Oribasos	One of ACTAEON'S hounds; the name means "mountain-ranger."
Orion	ARTEMIS'S hunter. After she killed him, he was placed in the sky as a constellation.
Orpheus	The greatest mortal musician. He journeyed to the Underworld to find his dead bride, EURYDICE.
Orthia	Another name for ARTEMIS.
Ossa	A mountain in THESSALY once inhabited by centaurs.
Otus	One of twin brothers, both giants, who wanted to prove themselves superior to the gods. ARTEMIS killed them for their presumption by making them accidentally kill each other.

Pachytos	One of ACTAEON'S hounds; the name means "thick-skinned."
Paean	The physician to the gods; also, APOLLO as healer.
Pales	The Strengthener of Cattle.
Palladium	The sacred image of ATHENA in TROY that protected the city as long as it was kept there.
Pamphagos	One of ACTAEON'S hounds; the name means "ravenous."
Pan	The God of the Goatherds and Shepherds who was part goat and part man.
Pandora	The first woman created by ZEUS; she brought evil into the world.
Panope	One of the sea nymphs.
Paphos	The daughter of the lovers PYGMALION and GALATEA, who gave her name to APHRODITE'S favorite city.
Paris	The TROJAN who kidnapped HELEN, starting the Trojan War.
Parthenon	ATHENA'S temple in Athens.
Pegasus	The winged horse that sprang from MEDUSA'S blood when PERSEUS killed her.
Peitho	The Goddess of Persuasion. She was the daughter of HERMES and APHRODITE.

Pelasgus — The ancestor of the Pelasgian—one of the earliest groups to inhabit the islands and mainland of Greece and Anaholia.

Peleus — ACHILLES' father. He was one of the ARGONAUTS.

Pelias — One of the twin sons of TYRO and POSEIDON.

Pelops — The son of TANTALUS. He was killed by his father, boiled in a cauldron, and served to the gods to eat.

Penates — The Gods of the Hearth and the Guardians of the Storehouse.

Penelope — ODYSSEUS'S faithful wife.

Pentheus — King of THEBES who was killed by the Bacchae when he was caught watching their secret rites.

Perdix — The nephew of Daedalus. When Perdix invented the saw and the compass, Daedalus became jealous and tried to kill Perdix. ATHENA saved him by changing him into a partridge.

Pergamos — The holy place of TROY.

Persephone — The Queen of the Underworld and wife of HADES.

Perseus — The hero who killed MEDUSA and was the faithful husband of ANDROMEDA.

Phaedra — ARIADNE'S sister and wife of THESEUS. When she fell in love with his son, HIPPOLYTUS, she killed herself.

Phaëthon — The son of APOLLO, whose wish to drive his father's chariot for one day almost led to the end of the world.

Phantasus | Variously, the son or brother of HYPNOS. Phantasus was the God of Dreams of Inanimate Objects.

Phaon | An old boatman to whom APHRODITE gave youth and beauty for ferrying her from Lesbos to Chios.

Philemon | A poor old man who with his wife was blessed by the gods, given a temple to live in, and promised that he would never live alone without her.

Philomela | PROCNE'S sister whose husband TEREUS pretended to marry Philomela, then cut out her tongue. The gods turned Philomela into a swallow.

Phineus | A prophet whom ZEUS cursed by having HARPIES defile his food whenever he wanted to eat.

Phobos | The God of Fear. He accompanied ARES into battle.

Phoebe | A TITAN who was the first Moon Goddess.

Pholus | A centaur-friend of Heracles (HERCULES).

Phrixus | The boy who was rescued from death by the ram with the GOLDEN FLEECE.

Pirene | Famous spring in Corinth.

Pittheus | King of Troezen and the father of THESEUS'S mother.

Pluto | The God of the Underworld. (See HADES.)

Plutus | The God of Wealth, a Roman allegorical figure.

Poena	The Roman Goddess of Punishment. The Greeks regarded her as an attendant of NEMESIS.
Pollux	The son of LEDA, who with his brother CASTOR was the Special Protector of Sailors.
Polybus	King of CORINTH, whom OEDIPUS believed was his father.
Polydeuces	Another name for POLLUX.
Polydorus	A son of PRIAM. According to Homer, he was killed by ACHILLES.
Polyidus	A wise seer of Corinth.
Polyxena	HECUBA'S daughter who was killed on ACHILLES' grave.
Pomenis	One of ACTAEON'S hounds; the name means "leader."
Pomona	The first NUMINA. She was later personified and became the Goddess of Gardens and Orchards.
Pontus	The God of the Deep Sea. He was a son of Mother Earth and the father of the Sea God NEREUS.
Porphyrion	A giant who rebelled against the gods.
Poseidon	The God of the Sea, who was CRONUS'S son and ZEUS'S brother.
Priam	King of TROY, during the war against the Greeks.
Priapus	The God of Fertility.

Procne	PHILOMELA'S sister, who avenged her sister's punishment by killing her own son and feeding him to her husband, TEREUS. The gods changed her into a nightingale.
Procris	The niece of PROCNE and PHILOMELA, who was accidentally killed with her husband's javelin.
Procrustes	A man who tied his victims onto an iron bed and cut or stretched them to fit on the bed. THESEUS killed Procrustes in the same manner.
Proetus	The king of ARGOS.
Prometheus	The Titan whose name means "forethought." He sided with ZEUS in his war with the TITANS.
Proserpine	Another name for PERSEPHONE.
Proteus	The god sometimes said to be POSEIDON'S son and sometimes said to be his attendant. Proetus could foretell the future and change his shape, at will.
Psyche	A beautiful maiden who married CUPID and was given immortality.
Psychopompus	Another name for HERMES.
Pterelas	One of ACTAEON'S hounds; the name means "winged."
Pygmalion	The sculptor who fell in love with his statue of a woman. APHRODITE brought the sculpture to life, as GALATEA, and the two were married.
Pylades	ORESTES' friend and cousin who helped avenge Agamemnon's murder.
Pylos	NESTOR'S home.

Pyramus	The beautiful youth who loved THISBE and killed himself because he thought she was dead. The red fruit of the mulberry is a memorial to the lovers.
Pyrrha	One of two people saved from the Flood that destroyed the world.
Python	A serpent killed by APOLLO.
Remus	One of the twin brothers who founded Rome. As children, they were washed ashore by the Tiber and saved by a she-wolf who fed them her milk. (See ROMULUS.)
Rhea	CRONUS'S sister-queen. She was the mother of ZEUS, POSEIDON, HADES, DEMETER, HERA, and HESTIA.
Rhesus	The TROJANS' Thracian ally, whose horses surpassed all mortal ones.
Romulus	REMUS'S twin brother who helped found Rome. (See REMUS.)
Salmoneus	A man who pretended to be ZEUS. The god struck him down with a lightning bolt.
Sarpedon	The son of ZEUS and EUROPA. He fought with the TROJANS against the Greeks.
Saturn	The Roman name for CRONUS.
Satyrs	Goat-men who were followers of PAN.
Scamander	The name used by mortals for the great river of TROY (called Xanthos by the gods).

Scheria	The country of the Phaeacians in the Odyssey.
Sciron	A man who made those he captured kneel to wash his feet and then would kick them down to the sea. THESEUS threw him over a precipice.
Scorpio	The scorpion, one of the signs of the Zodiac.
Scylla	A sea nymph whom CIRCE changed into a monster with serpents and dogs' heads coming from her body. Scylla destroyed all sailors who passed her.
Scyros	The island where THESEUS died and ACHILLES disguised himself as a girl.
Selene	The Moon Goddess. Selene was one of ARTEMIS'S three forms.
Selli	The people who made bread from acorns in ZEUS'S sacred grove.
Semele	DIONYSUS'S mother whom ZEUS loved.
Sibyl	A prophetess who guided AENEAS to the Underworld.
Sidero	TYRO'S maid who married her husband and was killed by Tyro's son, PELIAS.
Sileni	Followers of DIONYSUS and PAN, who were part man and part horse.
Silenus	A jovial fat old man who was always drunk. He was said to be PAN'S brother or son.
Simois	One of the rivers of TROY.

Sinis	A man who killed people by fastening them to two pine trees bent down to the ground. When the lashings were cut, his victims were torn limb from limb. THESEUS killed Sinis in the same manner.
Siren	One of the creatures with beautiful voices who lived on an island in the sea and lured sailors to their deaths.
Sirius	The Dog Star in the constellation Canis Major.
Sol	The Roman God of the sun.
Sphinx	The creature shaped like a winged lion with the breast and face of a woman. She beseiged THEBES until OEDIPUS answered her riddle.
Sterope	One of ATLAS'S daughters who was placed in the heavens as a star.
Stricta	One of ACTAEON'S hounds; the name means "spot."
Styx	The river of the unbreakable oath in the Underworld. Anyone who broke such an oath was banished from the council of the gods and denied nectar and ambrosia.
Sylvanus	One of the NUMINA; the Helper of Plowmen and Woodcutters.
Syracuse	The greatest city of Sicily.
Syrinx	A nymph loved by PAN. Her sister nymphs turned her into a tuft of reeds to save her from him, but he made the reeds into a pipe.
Talus	Last of the Bronze race. Talus was made completely of bronze except for one ankle.

Tantalus	ZEUS'S son whom the gods loved. Tantalus hated the gods and served them his son to eat. They discovered his treachery and punished him by putting him in HADES in a pool that drained whenever he tried to drink. They also placed fruit trees above him from which he could never pick fruit.
Tartarus	Another name for the Underworld.
Telamon	The father of AJAX. He was one of the ARGONAUTS.
Telemachus	The son of ODYSSEUS.
Telephus	Heracles' (HERCULES') son. He fought with the Greeks against the TROJANS.
Tempe	A beautiful valley near Mount Olympus.
Tereus	PROCNE'S husband. He was changed into a hawk.
Terminus	A NUMINA who was the Guardian of Boundaries.
Thalia	The MUSE of Comedy. She was also one of the three Graces.
Thamyris	A poet who was struck blind when he challenged the MUSES to a contest.
Thea	A TITAN who married her brother Hyperion and gave birth to the sun.
Thebes	The city founded by Cadmus.
Themis	Right or Divine Justice which sat beside ZEUS in OLYMPUS.
Theridamas	One of ACTAEON'S hounds; the name means "beast-tamer."

Theron — One of ACTAEON's hounds; the name means "savage-faced."

Theseus — The greatest Athenian hero.

Thespian Lion, The — A lion that ravaged livestock around Mount Cithaeron until Heracles (HERCULES) killed it.

"Ate"—Goddess of Mischief

Thessaly	The site of Mount OLYMPUS in northeastern Greece.
Thestius	A king of Calydon who was the father of LEDA and ALTHEA.
Thetis	The sea nymph who was the mother of ACHILLES.
Thisbe	PYRAMUS'S lover who killed herself after she found him dead. The red fruit of the mulberry tree is a memorial to them.
Thoös	One of ACTAEON'S hounds; the name means "swift."
Thrace	The home of a fierce people in the northeast of Greece.
Tiber	The God of the Tiber River, who instructed AENEAS to go to the site of Rome.
Titan	The elder gods who were huge and strong and ruled over the universe before ZEUS dethroned them.
Tityus	A giant killed by APOLLO and ARTEMIS.
Triton	The Trumpeter of the Sea. He was a son of POSEIDON.
Trivia	Another name for HECATE.
Trojan	An inhabitant of the city of TROY. (See also TROJAN in Chapter 5).
Troy	A wealthy city on the east end of the Mediterranean, where the Trojan War was fought.
Turnus	The king of the Rutulians who was one of LAVINIA'S suitors and consequently battled against AENEAS for her. Turnus lost his life.

Tyche	The Greek name for the Goddess of Fortune.
Tydides	Another name for DIOMEDES.
Tyndaris	The daughter of Tyndareus and LEDA.
Typhoeus	Another name for TYPHON.
Typhon	The monster with a hundred heads whom ZEUS conquered.
Tyro	The woman who bore POSEIDON twin sons, PELIAS and NELEUS.
Ulysses	Another name for ODYSSEUS.
Urania	The MUSE of Astronomy.
Uranis	One of ACTAEON'S hounds; the name means "heavenly one."
Uranus	The father of CRONUS, the TITANS, the CYCLOPS, and the Furies.
Venus	The Roman name for APHRODITE.
Vesper	Another name for HESPER.
Vesta	The Roman name for HESTIA.
Victoria	The Roman name for NIKE.
Virbius	The Roman name for HIPPOLYTUS.
Voluptas	The Roman Goddess of Pleasure.

Vulcan   The Roman name for HEPHAESTUS.

Xanthus   The gods' name for TROY'S great river.

Zephyr   The God of the West Wind.

Zetes   One of the ARGONAUTS.

Zethus   The twin brother of Amphion. Together, they built a wall around THEBES
                to fortify it.

Zeus   The Supreme God of the Universe.

"Moses"

CHAPTER **7**

Religious Names

All things bright and beautiful,
All creatures great and small,
All things wise and wonderful,
The Lord God made them all.

Cecil Frances Alexander
from *All Things Bright and Beautiful*

This chapter contains names from the world's major religions. Most of the suggestions are from the Judeo-Christian tradition—particularly the Old and New Testaments; but many are derived from Hindu, Buddhist, or Islamic scriptures and related sources.

Religious Names

Aaron	MOSES' brother whose rod became a serpent, when he cast it before Pharaoh. Aaron and his sons became the first priests of the Tabernacle.
Abednego	One of DANIEL'S three friends who survived the fiery furnace.
Abel	The son of ADAM and EVE. Abel's brother, CAIN, murdered him.
Abraham	The founder of the Hebrew people.
Absalom	A son of King DAVID who led a revolt against his father.
Adam	The first man created by God.
Agni	The Hindu fire god.
Ahab	The seventh king of the Northern Kingdom who married JEZEBEL. She persuaded him to abandon the worship of God for BAAL, the pagan deity.
Amalek	Esau's grandson who founded a warlike tribe that fought the Israelites.
Amos	A Hebrew prophet.
Ananias	An early Jewish Christian. When he and his wife lied to God, PETER denounced them, and they died.
Andrew	The brother of PETER who was one of the first disciples of Jesus.
Anna	A Hebrew prophetess who worshiped the infant Jesus.
Annas	The High Priest CAIAPHAS's father-in-law. When Jesus appeared before him after his arrest, Annas sent him to Caiaphas.

Antipas	One of Herod's sons who ruled Galilee and Perea during Jesus' lifetime. Antipas ordered JOHN THE BAPTIST beheaded.
Archelaus	One of Herod's sons who ruled Judea when JOSEPH (2), MARY (see MARY THE VIRGIN), and Jesus returned from Egypt.
Asenath	The wife of JOSEPH (1) who bore him two sons, Manasseh and EPHRAIM.
Baal	A pagan god worshiped in Phoenicia and Canaan whom some of the Israelites began to worship, angering God.
Barabbas	The robber whom PONTIUS PILATE released instead of Jesus.
Barak	The leader of Israel's forces against the Canaanite forces of King Jabin.
Barnabas	An early convert to Christianity who with PAUL preached the Gospel of Jesus.
Bartholomew	One of the Twelve Apostles, also known as NATHANAEL in one of the Gospels.
Bartimaeus	A blind beggar whose faith in Jesus restored his sight.
Bast	The Egyptian Goddess of Matrimony and Feminine Sensuality. Bast was originally represented as a cat.
Beelzebub	A pagan god whom the Philistines worshiped. He is sometimes identified with Satan.
Belshazzar	The Babylonian ruler for whom DANIEL interpreted the significance of the handwriting on the wall.

Religious Names

Benjamin	The youngest of Jacob's and Rachel's twelve sons.
Boaz	RUTH's second husband to whom she bore a son named Obed.
Brahma	The supreme Hindu deity, called Creator of the Worlds.
Buddha (Guatama)	The founder of Buddhism, which holds that suffering is inherent in life but that one can rise beyond it by mental and moral self-purification.
Caiaphas	The High Priest, a friend of the Romans, who tried Jesus and then turned Him over to PONTIUS PILATE.
Cain	The first-born son of ADAM and EVE. He killed his brother, ABEL.
Caleb	MOSES' spy who reported on the Canaanites' strength.
Chilion	NAOMI's and ELIMELECH's son.
Chuza	The husband of JOANNA.
Cleopas	One of the two disciples with whom Jesus spoke on the way to Emmaus after the Resurrection.
Cornelius	A Roman centurion who saw a vision and then was baptized by PETER, thus becoming the first Gentile to convert to Christianity.
Cush	A son of HAM named after the land where his descendants lived.
Cyrus	The founder of the Persian Empire who released the Jews and told them to return to Jerusalem.
Dagon	One of the Philistines' pagan gods.

Dalai Lama	The spiritual leader of the Tibetan and Mongolian branch of Buddhism.
Daniel	Israel's great prophet whom God delivered from the lions' den.
Darius	The Babylonian king who cast DANIEL to the lions because of his great love for God.
David	The boy who slew the giant GOLIATH and went on to become the greatest of Israel's kings. He built the city of Jerusalem.
Deborah	A prophetess who helped BARAK defeat the Canaanites.
Delilah	SAMSON'S love who betrayed him to the Philistines.
Demas	An early Christian who accompanied PAUL during his first Roman imprisonment.
Demetrius	A silversmith who incited a riot against PAUL because the latter's preaching had ruined the man's sale of silver models of the temple of the goddess Diana.
Dinah	A daughter of JACOB and Leah.
Dionysius	An Athenian whom PAUL converted and who became the first bishop of Athens.
Dorcas	Another name for Tabitha, a woman disciple whom PETER raised from the dead.
Drusilla	A daughter of Herod Agrippa I.
Eleazar	One of AARON'S sons who became High Priest after his father's death.

Eli	The priest at Shiloh. Hannah brought her son SAMUEL to him.
Elijah	A great prophet of Israel who opposed AHAB and Queen JEZEBEL by fighting against the worship of the BAAL.
Elimelech	NAOMI'S husband and father of RUTH'S first husband, Mahlon.
Elisabeth	The mother of JOHN THE BAPTIST and a cousin of Mary (see MARY THE VIRGIN), the mother of Jesus.
Elisha	The prophet who succeeded ELIJAH.
Elkanah	The husband of HANNAH who was the father of the prophet SAMUEL.
Enoch	CAIN's eldest son.
Epaenetus	The first Greek convert to Christianity.
Epaphras	An early Christian friend of PAUL.
Ephraim	JOSEPH's second son. Part of Canaan was named for him.
Erastus	One of PAUL's attendants who went as a missionary into Macedonia.
Esau	ISAAC's eldest son who sold his birthright to his brother JACOB for a bowl of lentils.
Esther	A Hebrew orphan girl who married Ahasuerus (Xerxes), the King of Persia, and consequently was able to save her people from persecution.
Eutychus	A young man who fell from a window while listening to PAUL. The apostle restored his life.

Eve	The first woman created by God.
Ezekiel	A major Hebrew prophet.
Ezra	A Hebrew priest and scholar.
Felix	The Roman procurator who tried PAUL.
Gabriel	The archangel who announced the birth of Christ to the Virgin Mary (see MARY THE VIRGIN) and told her what to name Him.
Gad	The son of JACOB and Zilpah who founded one of the Twelve Tribes of Israel.
Gedaliah	The Hebrew governor appointed by NEBUCHADNEZZAR.
Gehazi	The Prophet ELISHA's servant who was cursed with leprosy for betraying his master.
Gershon	One of the three grandsons of JACOB who accompanied him to Eygpt.
Gideon	One of the great judges of Israel, whom God chose to free the Children of Israel from the threat of the Midianites and other hostile tribes.
Goliath	The giant whom DAVID killed.
Habakkuk	A minor Hebrew prophet.
Hagar	SARAH's handmaid. She was the mother of ISHMAEL, who is regarded as the ancestor of the Arabs.
Haggai	A minor Hebrew prophet.

Religious Names

Ham	One of NOAH'S sons. Ham is considered the ancestor of all black Africans.
Hamutal	The mother of two kings—Jehoahaz and Zedekiah.
Hannah	The mother of SAMUEL, the judge and prophet.
Hanuman	The monkey god in Hindu mythology.
Heman	A musician and dancer and the grandson of the prophet SAMUEL. Heman sang and played in the temple during the reign of King DAVID.
Hephzibah	Wife of King HEZEKIAH. The name means "my delight is in her."
Herodias	Herod Antipas's wife who actually was instrumental in the death of JOHN THE BAPTIST.
Hezekiah	A king of Judah who reclaimed some of his nation's lands from the Philistines.
Hilkiah	A high priest who discovered the lost *Book of the Law*, or *Deuteronomy*.
Hophni	ELI'S son who, with his brother, died in battle, losing the Ark of the Covenant to the Philistines.
Hosea	A minor prophet.
Hur	A Hebrew who stood by MOSES during the battle with AMALEK.
Ichabod	The grandson of ELI.
Indra	The Hindu Rain God, the King of heaven.

Isaac	ABRAHAM's son whom Abraham almost sacrificed to God to prove his faith. Isaac married REBEKAH, and they had two sons, ESAU and JACOB.
Isaiah	Generally regarded as the greatest Hebrew prophet.
Ishmael	Abraham's son by HAGAR, his wife's handmaid. Ishmael founded a great nation of people in Arabia, where the Muslims revere him.
Israel	The name given to JACOB by an angel, which the Twelve Hebrew Tribes later adopted.
Jacob	Son of ISAAC and REBEKAH, who wrestled with the angel of the Lord and consequently was named ISRAEL.
Jambavat	The Hindu King of the Bears.
James	(1) The son of Alphaeus who became one of the Twelve Apostles. (2) The Apostle who was the son of ZEBEDEE and the brother of JOHN.
Jehoshaphat	One of JUDAH's greatest kings, who tried to abolish paganism and who was a great military leader.
Jeremiah	A major Hebrew prophet.
Jesse	King DAVID's father.
Jezebel	The evil queen married to King AHAB. She persecuted the Israelites until chariot horses trampled her to death.
Joanna	One of Jesus' earliest followers.

Job	A man who suffered a long series of great miseries. His name has become synonymous with patience.
John	One of the Twelve Apostles. He is considered the author of *Revelations* and the *Gospel of John.*
John the Baptist	Jesus' forerunner.
Jonah	The Hebrew prophet who was swallowed by a whale because he did not want to go to Nineveh to preach. He repented and went to Nineveh.
Joseph	(1) One of JACOB'S and RACHEL'S sons. Joseph's jealous brothers sold him as a slave into Egypt. (2) The husband of Mary (see MARY THE VIRGIN), the mother of Jesus.
Joshua	An Israelite who after MOSES' death led his people in their first conquests in Canaan.
Judah	JACOB'S fourth son who founded the largest of the Twelve Tribes of Israel.
Judas Iscariot	The Apostle who betrayed Jesus to His enemies.
Jude	The son of Mary (see MARY THE VIRGIN) and JOSEPH, thus believed by some to be a brother of Jesus.
Kama	The Hindu God of Love.
Kasmir (or Katmir or Kitmir)	The dog, according to Muslim tradition, that was one of the animals Mohammed admitted to Paradise.
Krishna	An incarnation of VISHNU.

Lazarus	Jesus' friend and the brother of MARTHA and MARY OF BETHANY. Jesus raised Lazarus from the dead.
Levi	One of JACOB's sons. Levi founded one of the Twelve Tribes of Israel.
Lot	ABRAHAM'S nephew whom God saved, along with his family, from the destruction of Sodom.
Lucifer	The light-bearer; the star that brings in the day (the morning star). Originally an archangel, Lucifer led a rebellion, was cast out of heaven, and became identified with the Devil.
Luke	An early Christian who accompanied PAUL on two of his missionary journeys. The third gospel is attributed to Luke.
Lydia	A wealthy woman who was PAUL's first European convert.
Malachi	A prophet of Israel.
Mark	One of the Evangelists. He is considered the author of the *Gospel of Mark*.
Martha	The sister of LAZARUS and MARY OF BETHANY.
Mary Magdalene	A woman who was one of Jesus' devoted followers. She was one of the two women who discovered Jesus' empty tomb.
Mary of Bethany	The sister of MARTHA and LAZARUS, who anointed Jesus in Simon the Leper's house.
Mary the Virgin	The mother of Jesus and wife of JOSEPH.

Matthew	One of the Twelve Apostles whose original name was LEVI. The *Gospel of Matthew* is ascribed to him.
Matthias	The disciple chosen to take the place of JUDAS.
Mecca	The birthplace of MOHAMMED in Saudi Arabia and the Islamic holy city.
Meshach	One of DANIEL'S three companions who survived the fiery furnace.
Methuselah	A Biblical figure who was renowned for his longevity.
Meuzza	MOHAMMED'S beloved cat. She was one of the animals admitted to Islamic Paradise.
Micah	A minor Hebrew prophet.
Miriam	MOSES and AARON's sister who became a prophetess.
Mohammed	The founder of the Islamic religion.
Moses	The Hebrew prophet who led the Israelites out of Egypt and who received the Ten Commandments from God.
Naomi	The mother-in-law of RUTH.
Nathanael	One of the Twelve Apostles, known as BARTHOLOMEW in the first three Gospels.
Nebuchadnezzar	A powerful king of Babylon who invaded Israel several times, carrying its people into bondage and razing Jerusalem and the Holy Temple.

Nicodemus	A Pharisee who defended Jesus at one of His trials, and buried Him after the Crucifixion.
Noah	The builder of the ark who saved himself, his family, and two of each of the world's animals from the Flood.
Obadiah	A minor prophet.
Obed	The grandfather of King DAVID.
Paul	The first Christian missionary who had persecuted Christians until he saw a vision on the road to Damascus.
Peter	The Apostle who as a fisherman had been called SIMON (THE CANAANITE). Jesus changed his name to Peter, meaning "rock."
Philip	One of the Twelve Apostles.
Pontius Pilate	The Roman procurator of Judea who tried and condemned Jesus.
Ra	The Eygptian God of the Sun.
Rachel	The wife of JACOB'S and mother of his sons, JOSEPH and BENJAMIN.
Rama	The Hindu king who was the son of VISHNU, his incarnation on earth.
Ravan	The Hindu demon king.
Rebekah	The wife of ABRAHAM'S son ISAAC and mother of his sons, ESAU and JACOB.
Reuben	JACOB'S first son who founded one of the Twelve Tribes of Israel.

Ruth	The young woman whose story is told in the Old Testament *Book of Ruth*. She was the great-grandmother of King DAVID.
Samson	The strongest man in the Bible who received his strength from his long hair. His love, DELILAH, betrayed him.
Samuel	A prophet and judge of Israel who delivered the Israelites at Mizpah from Philistine oppression and who anointed SAUL as the first king of Israel.
Sarah	The wife of ABRAHAM.
Sarama	The great god INDRA's watchdog and messenger in Hindu mythology.
Sarameyau	SARAMA's savage twin sons in Hindu mythology, who guided the souls of the dead to their final resting place.
Saraswati	The Hindu Goddess of Speech.
Saul	The first king of Israel.
Seth	The third son of ADAM and EVE.
Shadrach	One of DANIEL's three companions who survived the fiery furnace.
Sheba (Queen of)	The wealthy queen who visited King SOLOMON.
Shiva	The great Hindu god whose third eye will destroy the world.
Simeon	A son of JACOB and LEAH, who founded one of the Twelve Tribes of Israel.
Simon (the Canaanite)	One of the Twelve Apostles.

Simon of Cyrene	The man who carried the cross for Jesus.
Sita	RAMA's wife, the ideal Hindu woman.
Solomon	King DAVID's son who became the third king of Israel and built the first temple.
Stephen	An early Christian. He was stoned to death for his beliefs, thereby becoming the first Christian martyr.
Thaddaeus	One of the Twelve Apostles. He is also called Jude and Lebbaeus.
Thomas	The Apostle known as "doubting Thomas" because he would not believe in the Resurrection until he saw Jesus' wounds.
Timothy	PAUL's friend and companion.
Titus	PAUL's Greek assistant and companion, who was converted by him.
Tobit's Dog	(1) One of the animals placed in Islamic Paradise. (2) The dog who appears in the *Book of Tobit* in the Apocrypha to the Bible.
Varuna	The Hindu God of the Waters.
Vayu	The Hindu God of the Wind.
Vishnu	The great Hindu god who preserves the three worlds.
Yama	The Hindu God of Death.
Zacharias	A priest who was the father of JOHN THE BAPTIST.

Religious Names

Zebedee — The father of the two apostles JAMES and JOHN.

Zechariah (or Zachariah) — A priest and minor Hebrew prophet whose visions and teachings appear in the Old Testament that bears his name.

Zephaniah — A minor prophet of Israel whose teachings appear in the Old Testament named for him.

Zoroaster — A Persian religious teacher, the founder of the Zoroastrian religion.

CHAPTER **8**

Royalty and Titles

I'll call thee Hamlet,
King, father, Royal Dane: Oh, answer me!

William Shakespeare
from *Hamlet*

No better way exists to exalt your pet and show your high esteem than by giving it a prestigious title. Most of the names in this section are royal designations, but quite a few are military or civil.

Royalty and Titles

Admiral	Cadet	Corporal	Detective
Airman	Captain	Counselor	Director
Ambassador	Chancellor	Count	Doctor
Baron	Chief	Countess	Duchess
Baroness	Coach	Czar (Tsar)	Duke
Brigadier (General)	Colonel	Czarina (Tsarina)	Earl
Brother	Commander	Dean	Emperor

"Pasha"

Empress
Ensign
General
Governor
Highness
Inspector
Judge
Kaiser
Khan
King
Knight
Lady
Lieutenant
Lord
Madame

Mademoiselle
Majesty
Major
Master
Matriarch
Mayor
Midshipman
Minister
Miss
Mister
Mistress
Monsieur
Ms.
Officer
Pasha

Patriarch
Pharaoh
Preacher
Premier
President
Prime Minister
Prince
Princess
Private
Queen/Queenie
Rabbi
Representative
Reverend
Rex
Rey

Ruler
Seaman
Secretary
Senator
Senior
Señor
Señorita
Sergeant
Shah
Sheik
Shogun
Sir
Sister
Squire
Teacher

"McDuff"

CHAPTER 9

Foreign Words and Names

A man who is ignorant of foreign languages is ignorant of his own.

Johann von Goethe

If you have a flair for the exotic, or simply want to impress your friends with your multilingual skills, then the names in this chapter will intrigue you and possibly prompt you to open a foreign language dictionary. Your best choice is a pleasant sounding word, preferably one you can pronounce correctly, and one with a translation that appropriately fits your pet. For instance, be careful not to embarrass yourself and your black cat by naming him Amarillo, the Spanish word for "yellow"!

Foreign Words and Names

Agape	Greek for word meaning "love."
Allegre	Spanish for "happy."
Aloha	Hawaiian word for "hello" or "goodbye."
Amarillo(a)	Spanish for "yellow." Use Amarillo for a male and Amarilla for a female.
Amigo(a)	Spanish word meaning "friend." Use Amigo for a male and Amiga for a female.
Amore	Italian for "love."
Astra	Latin for "star."
Azul	Spanish for "blue."
Beau/Belle	French for "handsome/beautiful" (male/female).
Bébé	French for "baby."
Beeren	German for "berries."
Bianca Pinjarra	Some of the crown jewels of England.
Bianco(a)	Italian for "white." Use Bianco for a male and Bianca for a female.
Bier	German word for "beer."
Bijou	French for "jewel."
Blanco(a)	Spanish for "white." Use Blanco for a male and Blanca for a female.

Blanquito(a)	Spanish for "little white one." Use Blanquito for a male and Blanquita for a female.
Bleu/Bleue	French for "blue" (male/female).
Bobae	Korean for "Heirloom."
Bonito(a)	Spanish for "pretty." Use Bonito for a male and Bonita for a female.
Canela	Spanish for "cinnamon."
Caro/Cara	Italian for "dear" (male/female). Gaelic for "friend."
Celia	"Little heavenly one."
Chansu	Japanese for "chance."
Chat	French for "cat."
Chatool	Hebrew for "cat."
Chico	Spanish for "young man."
Chien	French for "dog."
Chiquita	Spanish for "little girl."
Coeur	French for "heart."
Concha	Spanish for "shell."
Diablo	Spanish for "devil."

Foreign Words and Names

Dolce	Italian for "sweet."
Dono	Italian for "gift."
Faeden	Gaelic for "golden."
Faux Pas	French for "a social blunder."
Felice	Italian for "happy."
Feliz	Spanish for "happy."
Feo	Spanish for "ugly."
Fiesta	Spanish for "party."
Flavo	Italian for "fair or blonde."
Fraulein	German for "young woman."
Freida	A German name for a female.
Frieden	German for "peace."
Frijol	Spanish for "bean."
Fritz	A German name for a male.
Gato (2)	Spanish for "cat." Use Gato for a male and Gata for a female.
Gigio	Italian for "cricket."

Greta	A German name for a female.
Gretchen	A German name for a female.
Gretel	A German name for a female.
Gris	Spanish for "gray."
Hans	A German name for a male.
Heidi	A German name for a female.
Heinrich	A German name for a male; it translates as "Henry."
Hombre	Spanish for "man."
Hummel	A German name for a male.
Ilsa	A German name for a female.
José	A Spanish name for a male.
Kannika	"Jasmine-like blossom" in Japanese.
Katarina (Katrina)	A Russian name for a female.
Keseff	Hebrew for "silver."
Klein	German for "small."
Kochka	Russian for "cat."

Foreign Words and Names

Kui — Hawaiian for "roar."

Kut — The Egyptian name for the male cat.

Kutta — The Egyptian name for the female cat.

Laddie — Scottish for "young man."

Lassie — Scottish for "young woman."

Lieb — German for "dear."

Liesel — A German name for a female.

Linda — Spanish for "pretty."

Luna — Spanish for "moon."

Madame — French for "Mrs. or Madam."

Mademoiselle — French for "Miss."

Mar — Spanish for "sea."

Marta — A German name for a female.

McCloud — A Scottish name.

McDuff — A Scottish name.

McMurphy — A Scottish name.

"*Sushi*"

McTavish	A Scottish name.
Mesa	Spanish for "table."
Mi	Spanish for "my."
Misha	A Russian name for a male.
Monique	A French name for a female.
Monsieur	French for "Mister."
Muñeca	Spanish for "doll."
Natasha	A Russian name for a female.
Nicole	A French name for a female.
Nikko	Japanese for "cat."
Octavia/n	A Latin name for a female/male.
Omar	A Middle Eastern name.
Oso(a)	Spanish for "bear." Use Oso for a male and Osa for a female.
Paco	A Spanish name for a male.
Pancho	A Spanish name for a male.
Pepe	A Spanish name for a male.

Perro (a)   Spanish for "dog." Use Perro for a male and Perra for a female.

Poco   Spanish for "little."

Renée   A French name.

Rio   Spanish for "river."

Rojo(a)   Spanish for "red." Use Rojo for a male and Roja for a female.

Rosita   A Spanish name for a female.

Sasha   A Russian name.

Sayonara   Japanese for "goodbye."

Schnell   German for "fast" or "quick."

Schotzie   A German name.

Señor   Spanish for "Mister."

Señorita   Spanish for "Miss."

Simba   African for "lion."

Som Phong   Tai word meaning "like one's ancestors."

Suki   A Japanese name.

Summa   Latin for "the most."

Sushi	Japanese for "raw fish."
Taiko	Japanese for "boss."
Tanya	A Russian name for a female.
Tasha	A Russian name for a female. (Short for Natasha.)
Tigre (a)	Spanish for "tiger." Use Tigre for a male and Tigra for a female.
Toro	Spanish for "bull."
Toutou	French for "doggie."
Trinka	A German name for a female. (Short for Katrinka.)
Vaquero	Spanish for "cowboy."
Wolfgang	A German name for a male.

"Faux Pas"

"Puss in Boots"

CHAPTER 10

Literature and Art

Ghastly grim and ancient Raven wandering
from the nightly shore—
Tell me what thy lordly name is on the
Night's Plutonian shore!
Quoth the raven, "Nevermore."

Edgar Allan Poe
from *The Raven*

Some of the most memorable animals are those that appear in literature and art. This chapter includes many of those animals, particularly dogs and cats, as well as a few famous human literary and artistic characters.

Adonis	Title character in the Shakespearan narrative poem *Venus and Adonis*.
Agatha Christie	The famous twentieth-century mystery writer.
Aladdin	The boy hero who releases a magic genie by rubbing a magic lamp in *The Thousand and One Nights*.
Alidoro	A mastiff in Carlos Collodi's (Lorenzini) *Pinocchio* (1883). Pinocchio saved Alidoro from drowning; in return Alidoro rescued the puppet from being fried like a fish when coated with flour.
Ann	One of the bluetick hounds of the pair Ann and DAN in the book *Where the Red Fern Grows* by Wilson Rawls.
Antony (Mark)	(Marcus Antonius, 83?–30 B.C.) Triumvir in Rome with Octavian and Marcus Aemilius Lepidus after the murder of Julius Caesar. Also a character in the Shakespearean plays *Antony and Cleopatra* and *Julius Caesar*.
Appollinaris	A cat that belonged to Mark Twain.
Ariel	A delicate spirit in the Shakespearean play *The Tempest*.
Aristophanes	A Greek comedy writer during the last half of the fifth and first half of the fourth centuries B.C. He refers to the myths in his works.
Ashley	The master of Twelve Oaks in Margaret Mitchell's classic novel *Gone With the Wind* (1936).
Aurora	A character from Jimmy Buffett's *Tales from Margaritaville*.

Banshee | A female spirit in Gaelic folklore whose appearance or wailing warns a family of the approaching death of one of its members.

Barge | In *The Fireside Book of Dog Stories* (1943), James Thurber tells of Barge, a watchdog who lived with a family in Columbus, Ohio. Barge took to drinking and neglected his duties until he came home one day and found that burglars had broken into his house. In despair and shame, Barge jumped out of a window and killed himself.

Baron | A dachshund in the book *Park Avenue Vet,* written by Louis J. Camuti.

Basket | Gertrude Stein's two dogs of the same name. They are described in works that Stein wrote in France during the period of the German occupation (1940–1945).

Ben | A dog described by Maxwell Knight, in *My Pet Friends*.

Beowulf | The hero of the Anglo-Saxon epic poem *Beowulf*.

Bevis | A large hound that was a prominent figure in Sir Walter Scott's novel *Woodstock* and was characterized after his own Scottish deerhound.

Big Red | The $7,000 Irish setter in Jim Kjelgaard's *Big Red* (1945). Big Red ruined his chances to be a show dog when he injured himself fighting a wolverine and a bear, thereby saving his master Danny Pickett.

Bilbo Baggins | One of the hobbits in J. R. Tolkien's novels.

Bion | An Alexandrian pastoral poet who wrote of the myths, around 250 B.C.

Blackie | A black spaniel that was Ernest Hemingway's companion for twelve years.

Blanche

One of the dogs that does not appear on stage but is mentioned in Act 3, Scene 6 of SHAKESPEARE'S play *King Lear* (1608).

Boatswain

Lord Byron's Newfoundland and the subject of a moving epitaph by the well-known poet.

Bodger

The old bull terrier in Sheila Burnford's *The Incredible Journey* (1961). Bodger was one of the three pets who faced tremendous hardships while traveling home through the Canadian wilderness.

Bond (James)

The main character and British spy in the popular Ian Fleming fictional series.

Boring Alice

A character from Jimmy Buffett's *Tales from Margaritaville*.

Brownie

The female Irish setter owned by T. H. White, the author of *The Once and Future King* (1958). White described his love for Brownie in his letters to David Garnett.

Buck

The large, powerful, mix-breed dog in Jack London's *The Call of the Wild*. Stolen from his home in California to be sold as a sled dog in Alaska, Buck was "beaten but not broken." He eventually joined a pack of wolves who signaled their acceptance of Buck by sniffing noses and howling at the moon.

Bull's-eye

The white shaggy mutt in Charles Dickens's *Oliver Twist* (1839). Bull's-eye belonged to the murderer, Bill Sikes, and had as unpleasant a disposition as his owner.

Bunyan (Paul)

The mythical lumberjack hero of the American West.

Cadpig	The smallest and prettiest of Pongo's fifteen puppies in Dodie Smith's *The Hundred and One Dalmatians* (1956). Cad pig's favorite pastime is watching television.
Caesar (Julius)	The powerful Roman political and military leader (100–44 B.C.) who was eventually murdered by Brutus.
Caliban	A character in the Shakespearean play *The Tempest*.
Catarina	A large tortoiseshell cat that belonged to Edgar Allan Poe and his wife Virginia. Catarina would lie on Virginia to keep her warm when Virginia was bedridden.
Catfish	Columnist Lewis Grizzard's dog who, as Grizzard reports in his column, liked to drink out of the toilet.
Charley	The large French poodle that accompanied John Steinbeck on his trip through the United States in the 1960s. Steinbeck recalls their adventures in *Travels with Charley* in which Charley is described as being his ambassador when meeting strange people.
Charlotte	A spider, the title character in *Charlotte's Web* by E. B. White. She saves the life of WILBUR the pig.
Chaucer (Geoffrey)	The greatest English poet of the Middle Ages who is best known for his classic, *The Canterbury Tales*.
Cheshire Cat, The	The famous grinning cat whom Alice encounters during her journey in *Alice's Adventures in Wonderland* (1865) by Lewis Carroll. (See also *Cheshire Cat* in Chapter 11.)

Cinderella	The girl who marries Prince Charming in the well-known fairy tale *Cinderella*.
Clarissa	A dog in James Thurber's *How to Name A Dog*.
Clifford	Title character of Norman Bridwell's children's book, *Clifford the Big Red Dog*.
Columbine	A stock character in early Italian comedy and pantomime. Columbine was the daughter of Pantaloon and the sweetheart of HARLEQUIN.
Cotton-Tail	The brother of FLOPSY and MOPSY. These three were the "good little bunnies [who] went down to the lane to gather blackberries," from Beatrix Potter's *The Tale of Peter Rabbit*.
Cujo	The canine title character of a Stephen KING novel.
Da Vinci (Leonardo)	The renowned Italian painter, artist, sculptor and architect (1452–1519).
Damn Spot	From SHAKESPEARE'S *Macbeth* (published in 1623), in which Lady Macbeth proclaimed: "Out, out, Damn spot" while walking through the castle distraught over the blood on her garment after killing her husband.
Dan	Half of the pair ANN and Dan in the book *Where the Red Fern Grows*.
Dante (Alighieri)	One of the greatest medieval poets. Dante's major literary work was *The Divine Comedy*.
Dash	A mongrel dog that belonged to writer Charles Lamb. Dash had once belonged to poet Thomas Hood. Lamb wrote about Dash's "crazy" behavior, which included the ability to stand on his hind legs.

Dash	Dashiell Hammett (1894–1961), an American crime novelist whose works include *The Maltese Falcon* and *The Thin Man*.
Dickens (Charles)	One of the most popular English novelists who criticized the wealthy and corrupt in nineteenth-century England.
Digit	A gorilla in the book *Gorillas in the Mist* by Diane Fosse (1983). He got his name from the fourth and fifth digits of his hand, which were webbed.
Dinah	Alice's cat, who was left behind when Alice fell down the rabbit-hole in Lewis Carroll's *Alice's Adventures in Wonderland* (1865).
Diogenes	The brutish dog that adored his owner, Florence Dombey, in Charles Dickens's *Dombey and Son* (1848).
Don Juan	One of the most famous literary figures in medieval legends. Don Juan has appeared in the works of Byron, Shaw, Moliere, and Mozart.
Dr. Watson	Sherlock Holmes's companion and the narrator of Sir Arthur Conan Doyle's (1859–1930) mystery books.
Duke	Penrod Schofield's dog. A scraggly, but faithful, companion in Booth Tarkington's *Penrod* (1914). (See also *Duke* in Chapter 5.)
El Dorado	The fictitious kingdom of untold wealth on the Amazon River for which Spanish and English explorers searched.
Emerson (Ralph Waldo)	American poet, essayist, and lecturer (1803–1882).

Euripides	A Greek tragic poet of the fifth century B.C., who wrote plays based on myths.
Feathers	Carl van Vechten's cat whose behavior he discussed in *The Tiger in the House* (1920).
Flicka	The title character in a novel about a horse, entitled *My Friend Flicka*.
Flopsy	One of the "good little bunnies" in Beatrix Potter's stories. (See COTTON-TAIL.)
Flossy	English writer Anne Bronte's fat little black-and-white spaniel.
Flush	Elizabeth Barrett Browning's red cocker spaniel. Elizabeth was holding Flush when she met Robert in Hodgson's Bookshop in 1846.
Fortitude	One of two lions whose statues guard the Fifth Avenue entrance to the main building of the New York Public Library. (See PATIENCE.)
Foss	Edward Lear's beloved tomcat for whom he created "The Heraldic Blazon of Foss the Cat," published in *Nonsense Songs, Stories, Botany and Alphabets*.
Frost (Robert)	One of America's greatest twentieth-century poets and winner of the Pulitzer Prize in 1924, 1931, 1937, and 1943 (1874–1965).
Fu Manchu	The villain in Sax Rohmer novels.
Gatsby (Jay)	A racketeer of the 1920s in F. Scott Fitzgerald's classic novel *The Great Gatsby* (1925).

Gipsy	The cat who left home to become an alley cat, in Booth Tarkington's *Penrod and Sam*.
Goldilocks	The little girl in the children's fairy tale *The Three Bears*.
Grendel	An anthropomorphic monster who ravaged Herot for twelve years and was killed by BEOWULF in the novel *Beowulf*.
Grimalkin	The demon spirit in the form of a cat mentioned by the First Witch in SHAKESPEARE'S *Macbeth* (1605).
Guinevere	KING ARTHUR'S wife in the stories of King Arthur and the Round Table.
Gulliver	Title character in Jonathan Swift's *Gulliver's Travels* (1726).
Hamlet	Title character of a Shakespearean play, published in 1603.
Harlequin	A clown in early Italian comedy and pantomime. Harlequin's tight-fitting costume has alternating patches of contrasting colors.
Hank the Cowdog	Title character of a children's book series by John R. Erikson.
Heidi	The heroine of *Heidi* by Johanna Spyri (1827–1901).
Hemingway (Ernest)	American novelist (1899–1936), 1954 winner of the Nobel Prize. Wrote *The Sun Also Rises, A Farewell to Arms, The Old Man and The Sea,* and *The Snows of Kilimanjaro,* among others.
Herodotus	The first historian of Europe. He refers to the myths in his works.
Hinse	The cat that belonged to the poet and novelist Sir Walter Scott of Edinburgh (1771–1832).

Holden	The main character in J. D. Salinger's novel *Catcher in the Rye* (1951).
Homer	The blind poet who wrote of the Greek myths in *The Iliad* and *The Odyssey*.
Horatio	Character in the Shakespearean play *Hamlet*.
Hound of the Baskervilles, The	The ghostly black hound that dwelt on the moors of Dartmoor and terrorized the Baskerville family in Sir Arthur Conan Doyle's *The Hound of the Baskervilles* (1902).
Jack	Title character in the Mother Goose nursery rhyme "Jack and Jill."
Jeannie	A Scotty that appears in *Thurber's Dogs* (1955).
Jennie	The discontented Sealyham terrier that became the star of the World Mother Goose Theatre in Maurice Sendak's *Higglety Pigglety Pop! or There Must Be More to Life* (1967).
Jill	Title character in the Mother Goose nursery rhyme "Jack and Jill."
Jip	(1) Dora Spenlow's small black spaniel who liked to walk on the dinner table in Charles Dickens's *David Copperfield* (1850). (2) The dog with an acute sense of smell that helped save a man stranded on an island in Hugh Lofting's *The Story of Doctor Dolittle* (1920).
Juliet	One of the star-crossed lovers in SHAKESPEARE'S *Romeo and Juliet* (1594–95).
Keeper	Emily Brontë's mastiff. When his mistress died, Keeper followed the coffin in the funeral procession and slept for nights at the door of her empty room.

Kiche | The she-wolf that whelped in Jack London's *White Fang* (1906).

King (Stephen) | A contemporary author of horror books, including *Carrie, The Shining, Pet Semetary* and *The Dead Zone*.

King Arthur | The legendary king of the Britons who restored order and peace in his kingdom. King Arthur's story is told in various literary works.

Kipling (Rudyard) | English poet, short story writer, and novelist (1865–1936); wrote *The Light that Failed* and *The Jungle Book,* as well as the well-known poem *Gunga Din*, among other works.

Lad | The thoroughbred collie who accomplished amazing deeds in Albert Payson Terhune's *Lad: A Dog* (1919). Terhune based Lad on his own collie, Sunnybank Lad.

Lady Godiva | The wife of Loefric, Earl of Mercia and Lord of Coventry. She rode naked through the town to get her husband to lower heavy taxes on the people. (c.1040–1080).

Lancelot | Sir Lancelot du Lac, the best of KING ARTHUR'S knights who loved Arthur's wife GUINEVERE in the stories of King Arthur and the Round Table.

Lassie | The collie in Eric Knight's pre-World War II short story "Lassie Come Home" (1938), who has since become a symbol of loyalty and dignity.

Lion of Lucerne, The (Lowendenkmal) | A statue of a dying lion erected in Lucerne's Glacier Garden to commemorate the Swiss Guards who were killed defending Louis XVI during the French Revolution.

Lobo
: The "King of Currumpaw," leader of a pack of wolves that attacked cattle in New Mexico. Ernest Thompson Seton wrote of his attempts to capture Lobo in *Wild Animals I Have Known* (1898). Seton finally succeeded by luring the wolf with the dead body of his mate, Blanca. (See BLANCA.)

Longfellow (Henry Wadsworth)
: The most popular and accomplished poet of the nineteenth century (1807–1882).

Lucian
: A second-century A.D. Greek writer who satirized the gods.

Lysander
: Character in the Shakespearean play *A Midsummer Night's Dream*.

Macavity
: The ginger cat that mysteriously disappears whenever anything turns up missing in "Macavity: the Mystery Cat" from *Old Possum's Book of Practical Cats* (1939) by T. S. Eliot.

Macbeth
: Title character of a Shakespearean play.

Marcellus
: Character in the Shakespearean play *Hamlet*.

Max
: A dachshund that is mentioned by Matthew Arnold in the elegy "Poor Matthias" (1882). See also MORITZ.

Merlin the Magician
: The legendary sorcerer who advised Arthur to establish the Round Table.

Merrylegs
: Jupe's performing circus dog in Charles Dickens's *Hard Times* (1854) who disappeared with his owner, only to return to the circus alone, lame, and almost blind.

Michelangelo
: The immensely talented Florentine painter, sculptor, architect, and poet (1475–1564) who was known, among other things, for his painting of the ceiling of the Sistine Chapel in Rome.

Minnaloushe	A black cat that is the subject of three verses in William Butler Yeats's *The Cat and the Moon* (1919).
Miss Muffet	The girl frightened by a spider in the popular nursery rhyme.
Mistigris	Madame Vauquer's cat in Honore de Balzac's *Le Père Goriot* (1835).
Mittens	The kitten who laughed so hard she fell off the wall in Beatrix Potter's *The Tale of Tom Kitten*.
Modigliani (Amedeo)	Italian painter and sculptor (1884–1920), who preferred oval and cylindrical shapes.
Mona Lisa	Leonardo Da Vinci's famous painting of the woman with the mysterious smile.
Monsieur Tibault	The cat that conducted a symphony orchestra with his tail in Stephen Vincent Benét's *The King of the Cats* (1929).
Moppet	One of the two kittens that "trod upon their pinafores and fell on their noses," in Beatrix Potter's *The Tale of Tom Kitten*.
Mopsy	One of the "good little bunnies" in Beatrix Potter's stories. (See COTTON-TAIL.)
Moritz	From *Max and Moritz,* the German classic by Wilhelm Busch. The names designate a pair of mischief-makers.
Morris	The famous finicky, striped tomcat of 9-Lives Cat Food commercials whose biography was written by Mary Daniels in 1974.
Mouschi	A cat that belonged to Ann Frank as described in *Diary of a Young Girl*.

Mozart (Wolfgang Amadeus)	Austrian composer who began to write music at the age of five. He wrote more than forty symphonies and twenty-two operas, among other great musical works.
Muggs	(1) The ferocious airedale in James Thurber's "The Dog That Bit People" from *My Life and Hard Times* (1933). (2) One of James Thurber's dogs included in his book, *Thurber's Dogs* (1955).
Music	The female greyhound described by William Wordsworth in the poem, "Incident Characteristic of a Favorite Dog" (1805). Music, who belonged to Mrs. Wordsworth's brother, tried desperately to save her friend Dart who had fallen through the ice on a lake. As she was breaking away the ice with her paws, Wordsworth described the scene: " . . . For herself she hath no fears Him alone she sees and hears."
Mutt	An amusing, black-and-white mongrel in Farley Mowat's *The Dog Who Wouldn't Be* (1957).
Nana	The Newfoundland dog that is the Darling children's nurse in J. M. Barrie's *Peter Pan* (1904).
Nero	Jane Welsh Carlyle's white terrier, part Maltese and part mongrel, who one day jumped from the library window, knocking himself senseless. Virginia Woolf relates the incident, claiming that perhaps the dog was attempting suicide, in *Flush* (1933).
Nox	The big black retriever whose behavior helped Father Brown solve Colonel Druce's murder in G. K. Chesterton's "The Oracle of the Dog" from *The Incredulity of Father Brown* (1926).

Octavian (Augustus) Julius Caesar's great-nephew (63 B.C.–A.D. 14).

Old Bob   The gray collie that was an award-winning sheepherder in *Bob, Son of Battle* (1898) by Alfred Ollivant.

Old Yeller   The rugged, stray yellow-gold dog who was adopted in Fred Gipson's *Old Yeller,* a novel about the Texas hill country in the frontier days of the 1860s. Old Yeller's name had a double meaning: the color of his hair coat and the yelling sounds he made.

Oliver (Twist)   The orphan in Charles Dickens's novel *Oliver Twist* (1837–39).

Othello   Title character of a Shakespearean play published in 1622.

Ovid   A Latin narrative poet who retold almost all of the stories of classical mythology.

Oz   From the novel *The Wonderful Wizard of Oz* (1900) by L. Frank Baum about Dorothy, a Kansas farm girl who was swept away by a tornado to the land of Oz.

Patience   One of two lions whose statues guard the Fifth Avenue entrance to the main building of the New York Public Library. (See FORTITUDE.)

Pepper   The names of three of Dandie Dinmont's six terriers (the other three were named MUSTARD) in Sir Walter Scott's *Guy Mannering* (1815).

Peter Rabbit   The mischievous little rabbit in Beatrix Potter's *The Tale of Peter Rabbit*. When Peter was hiding under a flower pot, he sneezed and was discovered by Mr. McGregor.

Phoebe   Holden's sister in J. D. Salinger's novel *Catcher in the Rye* (1951).

Picasso (Pablo) Famous Spanish artist and sculptor (1881–1973); the leading figure in modern art.

Pindar Greece's greatest lyric poet who alludes to the myths in all his poems.

Pinocchio The puppet whose nose grew when he lied in *Pinocchio* (1883) by Carlos Collodi (Lorenzini).

Professor Moriarity The arch enemy of Sherlock Holmes in Sir Arthur Conan Doyle's (1859–1930) mystery books.

Prynne (Hester) The main character in Nathaniel Hawthorne's 1850 novel *The Scarlet Letter*.

Puck A character in the Shakespearean play *A Midsummer Night's Dream*.

Puss in Boots The clever cat that was the sole inheritance a poor boy received from his father. The cat, who asked only for a pair of boots, tricked an ogre by challenging him to turn himself into a mouse. The cat ate the ogre, and his master took over the ogre's lands and castle.

Pyramus A character in the Shakespearean play *A Midsummer Night's Dream*.

Rab The powerful dog in Dr. John Brown's *Rab and His Friends* that kept a vigil at the bedside of his owner Ailie during her illness and subsequent death.

Raksha The Mother Wolf that raised Mowgli in Rudyard Kipling's *The Jungle Book* (1894).

Rembrandt A Dutch Baroque painter (1606–1669) whose works, including *The Night Watch*, have become treasured masterpieces.

Remus (Uncle)	The narrator of a series of stories by Joel Chandler Harris (1848–1908). Uncle Remus was a former slave who became a beloved family servant and who entertains a young boy by telling him animal stories.
Rhett	Rhett Butler, the irreverent Southerner who becomes Scarlett's third husband in Margaret Mitchell's *Gone With the Wind* (1936).
Rikki-Tikki-Tavi	The title character in RUDYARD KIPLING'S short story about a mongoose that fights cobras.
Rinnie	Nickname for *Rin Tin Tin*. (See Chapter 11.)
Romeo	One of the star-crossed lovers in SHAKESPEARE'S *Romeo and Juliet* (1594–95).
Rum Tum Tugger	A fictional cat in *Old Possum's Book of Practical Cats* by T. S. Eliot (1939).
Salinger (J. D.)	An American author (b. 1919), best known for his novel *Catcher in the Rye* (1951).
Savage Sam	OLD YELLER'S son in Fred Gipson's novel *Savage Sam* (1962).
Scarlett	The heroine of Margaret Mitchell's *Gone With the Wind* (1936).
Schuster	See SIMON.
Selima	Horace Walpole's tabby cat who was immortalized in a poem by Thomas Gray. Selima drowned in a goldfish bowl white trying to catch a fish. (Indeed, "curiosity killed the cat."!)

Sergeant Murphy	The brown dog that is a motorcycle-riding police officer in Richard Scarry's picture books.
Shakespeare (William)	(1564–1616) The English playwright who is known as history's greatest dramatist and the best English-language poet.
Shep	Shep, a collie that took care of a flock of sheep in New York City's Central Park, is described in an early twentieth-century story.
Sherlock Holmes	The famous detective in Sir Arthur Conan Doyle's (1859–1930) books.
Shimbleshanks	One of the cats in *Old Possum's Book of Practial Cats* by T. S. Eliot (1939).
Simon	Co-founder of Simon & SCHUSTER, a major New York publisher.
Simpkin	The tailor's cat in Beatrix Potter's *The Tailor of Gloucester* (1903).
Sinbad (the Sailor)	The sailor whose adventures include battling monsters in *The Arabian Nights*.
Sneakers	A cat about whom Margaret Wise Brown wrote in her *Seven Stories About a Cat Named Sneakers*.
Sophocles	A Greek playwright who wrote about the myths.
Sounder	The sharecropper's faithful dog with the resonant voice in William H. Armstrong's *Sounder* (1969).
Sour Mash	One of Mark Twain's several feline pets.

Stumpy	The big brown dog in Beatrix Potter's *The Tale of Little Pig Robinson* (1930).
Sweetheart	A dog referred to in Act 3, Scene 6 of SHAKESPEARE'S *King Lear* (1608).
Tabitha (Tabby)	A Siamese cat in *One Kitten Too Many* by Bianco Bradbury. Tabitha was called Tabby for short.
Tabitha Twitchit	The mother cat that was a shrewd businesswoman in Beatrix Potter's books.
Tailspin	The cat that was born on the moon in *Space Cat* by Ruthven Todd.
Tao	The male Siamese cat in *The Incredible Journey* (1961) by Sheila Burnford.
Tara	The O'Hara family's plantation in Margaret Mitchell's classic novel, *Gone With the Wind* (1936).
Tessa	A dog that belonged to author James Thurber.
Theocritus	An Alexandrian pastoral poet who wrote of the gods.
Tiger	The cat that played with KEEPER, the dog, in the household of Emily and Charlotte Brontë. (See also TIGER in Chapter 5.)
Tigger	The bouncy tiger in A. A. Milne's *The House at Pooh Corner* (1928).
Tinkerbell	The tiny fairy in *Peter Pan* (1904) by J. M. Barrie.
Titan (Tish-uhn)	One of the greatest painters of the Renaissance. This Italian master lived c. 1488–1576.

Toby	(1) A puppet dog in the Punch and Judy shows. (2) The ugly part spaniel who assists Sherlock Holmes and Dr. Watson in Sir Arthur Conan Doyle's *The Sign of Four* (1890).
Tom Kitten	The naughty kitten in Beatrix Potter's *The Tale of Tom Kitten* who was so fat his buttons burst off his clothes. He later lost his clothes, which were found by some ducks who wore them.
Tom Quartz	A kitten that President Theodore Roosevelt named for the fictional cat Tom Quartz in Mark Twain's book *Roughing It* (1872).
Toto	The dog that journeys with Dorothy in L. Frank Baum's *The Wonderful Wizard of Oz* (1900).
Toulouse-Lautrec (Henri de)	A leading postimpressionist artist whose works depicted the sordid late nineteenth-century Parisian society.
Tray	The dog in Thomas Campbell's poem "The Harper."
Van Gogh (Vincent)	The Dutch postimpressionist painter (1853–1890) whose works convey a wide spectrum of emotions.
Venus	Title character in the Shakespearean play *Venus and Adonis*.
Virgil	A Roman poet who wrote of the myths.
Wilbur	The pig in *Charlotte's Web* by E. B. White.
William	(1) Charles Dickens' (1812–1870) dear white cat, which he renamed Williamina when she had kittens. (2) The egotistical cat obsessed with his own name in James Thurber's "The Cat in the Lifeboat" from *Further Fables for Our Time* (1956).

Winnie-the-Pooh	The opinionated but delightful hero of A. A. Milne's stories about a teddy bear and his friends.
Wolf	The dog that accompanied Rip Van Winkle on the day that he fell asleep for twenty years (from Washington Irving's story of Rip Van Winkle).
Zoroaster	One of Mark Twain's several cats.

CHAPTER 11

Screen and Television

The play's the thing . . . !

William Shakespeare
from *Hamlet*

Who's the star of your household? Perhaps it's "Tonto," "Dracula," "Lassie," or maybe "Morris." Take your pick. But be careful; sometimes animals assume the characteristics of their namesakes. (Beware of "Pepe Le Pew.")

Abbott (Bud)	The sly con man in the Abbott and COSTELLO comedy team of the 1930s, '40s, and '50s.
Al Pacino	Academy Award winner, Best Actor, for his role in the movie, *Scent of a Woman* (1992).
Al	TIM'S "assistant" in the 1990s television series *Home Improvement*.
Alice Kramden	The wife of RALPH KRAMDEN, played by JACKIE GLEASON, in the 1950s television series *The Honeymooners*.
Amos	The character played by Alvin Childress on the television show *Amos 'n' Andy*.
Andy	The character played by Spencer Williams on the television show *Amos 'n' Andy*.
Anna Magnani	Academy Award winner, Best Actress, for her role in the movie, *The Rose Tattoo* (1955).
Anne Bancroft	Academy Award winner, Best Actress, for her role in the movie, *The Miracle Worker* (1962).
Anthony Hopkins	Academy Award winner, Best Actor, for his role in the movie, *The Silence of the Lambs* (1991).
Apollo	One of the two doberman pinschers owned by Robbin Masters on the television series *Magnum P.I.* (See ZEUS.)
Archie Bunker	The bigoted character played by Carroll O'Connor in the television series *All in the Family*.

Arnold	The pet pig in the television series *Green Acres* starring Eddie Albert and Eva Gabor.
Art Carney	Academy Award winner, Best Actor, for his role in the movie, *Harry and Tonto* (1974). Friend of RALPH KRAMDEN, played by JACKIE GLEASON, in the 1950s television series *The Honeymooners*.
Arthur	The drunken millionaire played by DUDLEY MOORE in the movie *Arthur*.
Asta	The wirehaired fox terrier in the television series *The Thin Man*. The Humane Association gave Asta two Patsy Awards for performing animals.
Audrey Hepburn	Academy Award winner, Best Actress, for her role in the movie, *Roman Holiday* (1953).
B. J. Honneycut	HAWKEYE'S buddy on the television series *M*A*S*H*.
Bagheera	The black panther in the Walt Disney movie *The Jungle Book* (1966).
Bailey	A character in the television series *Party of Five*.
Baloo	The bear in Walt Disney's movie *The Jungle Book* (1966).
Bam Bam	BARNEY and Betty Rubble's son in Hanna-Barbera's animated television cartoon *The Flintstones*.
Bambi	The fawn in Walt Disney's animated movie *Bambi* (1942).
Barbra Streisand	Academy Award winner, Best Actress, for her role in the movie, *Funny Girl* (1968).

Barnabas Collins	The vampire in the television series *Dark Shadows*.
Barnaby Jones	The private eye played by Buddy Ebsen in the television series *Barnaby Jones*.
Barney (Rubble)	The best friend of Fred Flintstone in Hanna-Barbera's animated television cartoon *The Flintstones*.
Barney Fife	The bungling deputy (1960–1965) in the television series *The Andy Griffith Show*.
Bart Maverick	One of the brothers, played by Jack Kelly, living in the frontier west in the television series *Maverick*.
Bashful	One of the Seven Dwarfs in the Walt Disney movie *Snow White and the Seven Dwarfs* (1937).
Batman	Batman first appeared in *Detective Comics* in May 1939. In the spring of 1940, *Batman Comics* evolved. The Mutual Radio Network also featured the voices of Batman and ROBIN during the 1940s. The ABC television series ran from 1966 until 1968. The first movie *Batman* (1989) featured Michael Keaton in the title role. The second movie, *Batman Returns* (1992), also starred Michael Keaton. The third movie, *Batman Forever* (1995), starred Val Kilmer.
Beaver (Cleaver)	The hapless younger son of the Cleavers in the television series *Leave It to Beaver*.
Beeswax	A cat in the 1989 Tom Selleck film *Her Alibi*.
Ben Kingsley	Academy Award winner, Best Actor, for his role in the movie, *Ghandi* (1982).

Benji

The shaggy mutt who became a star, appearing in *Benji* (1974), *For the Love of Benji* (1977), and *Oh Heavenly Dog* (1980).

Bert

One of the muppet characters in the television series *Sesame Street*. (See ERNIE and OSCAR THE GROUCH.)

Bette Davis

Academy Award winner, Best Actress, for her roles in the movies *Dangerous* (1935), and *Jezebel* (1938).

Binford

The name of the tool company in the 1990s television series *Home Improvement*.

Bing Crosby

Academy Award winner, Best Actor, for his role in the movie, *Going My Way* (1944).

Bloop Bloop

The extraterrestrial creature from the television series *Lost in Space* (1965–1968).

Bogart (or Bogey)

Humphrey Bogart, the famous actor, who starred in numerous films.

Bojangles (Bill Robinson)

A dancer and entertainer (1878–1949), appeared in SHIRLEY TEMPLE movies.

Boo-Boo Kitty

SHIRLEY'S stuffed cat in the television series *Laverne and Shirley*.

Bosley

The man who acts as an intermediary between the elusive Charlie and his female detectives in the television series *Charlie's Angels*.

Brady

The name of the family in the television series *The Brady Bunch*.

Brando (Marlon) | One of the most famous American actors after World War II. Brando won Academy Awards for his performances in *On the Waterfront* (1954) and *The Godfather* (1972).

Bret Maverick | One of the brothers, played by James Garner, living in the frontier west in the television series *Maverick*.

Brewster | The baseball player, played by Richard Pryor, who inherits a fortune in the movie *Brewster's Millions*.

Broderick Crawford | Academy Award winner, Best Actor, for his role in the movie, *All the King's Men* (1949).

Brubaker | The prison inspector played by Robert Redford in the movie *Brubaker*.

Bubba | The friend of FORREST GUMP in the Academy Award-winning (1994) movie *Forrest Gump* starring TOM HANKS.

Bud | A character played by Charlie Sheen in the movie *Wall Street*.

Buffy | The little blonde-haired girl in the television series *Family Affair*.

Bullet | Roy Rogers' German shepherd who debuted in the movie *Spoilers of the Plains* (1951) and later appeared on the *Roy Rogers Show*.

Burt Lancaster | Academy Award winner, Best Actor, for his role in the movie, *Elmer Gantry* (1960).

Burt Reynolds | Actor who has starred in a variety of movies in the 1960s, '70s, and '80s.

Butch Cassidy	The western outlaw played by PAUL NEWMAN in the 1969 movie *Butch Cassidy and the Sundance Kid.* (See SUNDANCE KID.)
Butkus	ROCKY'S dog in the original movie *Rocky.*
Car Face	The sinister gang leader "Junkyard Dog" in the 1989 animated cartoon *All Dogs Go to Heaven.*
Cat Ballou	The main character of the 1965 movie *Cat Ballou.*
Charles Laughton	Academy Award winner, Best Actor, for his role in the movie, *The Private Life of Henry VIII* (1932).
Charlie Chaplin	One of the most famous actors in motion picture history. Chaplin is best remembered for his roles in silent films.
Charlie	The lead character in the animated movie *All Dogs Go To Heaven* (1989).
Charlton Heston	Academy Award winner, Best Actor, for his role in the movie, *Ben Hur* (1959).
Cher	Academy Award winner, Best Actress, for her role in the movie, *Moonstruck* (1987).
Cheshire Cat	The grinning cat who fades away except for his grin. Created by Lewis Carroll, the Cheshire Cat appeared in Walt Disney's animated movie *Alice in Wonderland* (1951). (See also *Cheshire Cat* in Chapter 10.)
Chewbacca (or Chewy)	The 100-year-old "Wookie" in the movie *Star Wars* (1977) and its sequels.

Chinook	The white German shepherd who costarred with Kirby Grant in a series of movies about a Mountie and his dog (1949–1954). Chinook later played White Shadow in the *Mickey Mouse Club's* Corky and White Shadow serial.
Cinderella	The fairy-tale heroine who marries Prince Charming in Walt Disney's animated movie *Cinderella*.
Clarabelle	The puppet clown in the 1950s television series *Howdy Doody*.
Clark Gable	The popular American film star (1901–1960) once called "The King," best known for his role as Rhett Butler in the 1939 movie *Gone With the Wind*.
Clark Griswold	The lead character in the National Lampoon *Vacation* movie series starring Chevy Chase.
Claudette Colbert	Academy Award winner, Best Actress, for her role in the movie, *It Happened One Night* (1934).
Claw	The one-eyed foe of Combo in *Combo the White Lion*.
Cleo	The glum-faced basset hound who commented on the characters and events in the 1950s television show *The People's Choice*.
Cliff Robertson	Academy Award winner, Best Actor, for his role in the movie, *Charly* (1968).
Costello (Lou)	The rotund victimized member of the ABBOTT and Costello comedy team.
Curly	(1) One of the characters in the movie series *The Three Stooges*. (2) The tough trial boss played by Jack Palance in the movie *City Slickers*.

Daniel Day-Lewis   Academy Award winner, Best Actor, for his role in the movie, *My Left Foot* (1989).

Darth Vader   The commander of the forces of evil in the movie *Star Wars* (1977) and its sequels.

David Niven   Academy Award winner, Best Actor, for his role in the movie, *Separate Tables* (1958).

Diane Keaton   Academy Award winner, Best Actress, for her role in the movie, *Annie Hall* (1977).

Dickinson (Angie)   An actress who has starred in both television and movie roles, including the television series *Police Woman*.

Dobie Gillis   A romantically inclined teenage boy in the television series *The Many Loves of Dobie Gillis*. Dobie also appeared in the movie *The Affairs of Dobie Gillis* (1953).

Doc   One of the Seven Dwarfs in Walt Disney's animated movie *Snow White and the Seven Dwarfs* (1937).

Dolly (Parton)   The country western singer, song writer, and actress (*Nine to Five*). She appeared in her own television variety show *Dolly*. She also opened her own theme park, Dollywood, in Tennessee in 1986.

Dopey   One of the Seven Dwarfs in Walt Disney's animated movie *Snow White and the Seven Dwarfs* (1937).

Dracula   The vampire created by the novelist Bram Stoker, who first appeared in the 1931 movie *Dracula, The Un-Dead*.

Duchess	A Parisian cat in Walt Disney's animated movie, *The Aristocats* (1970). Duchess has a romance with O'Malley, the alley cat.
Dudley (Moore)	The contemporary comedian and movie star.
Duke	An airedale owned by famous Western actor John Wayne. The dog's name inspired Wayne's nickname, "The Duke."
Dustin Hoffman	Academy Award winner, Best Actor, for his roles in the movies, *Kramer vs. Kramer* (1979), and *Rain Man* (1988).
E. T.	The extraterrestrial being in Steven Spielberg's movie *E.T.*
Elaine	A character in the television series *Seinfeld*.
Elizabeth Taylor	Academy Award winner, Best Actress, for her roles in the movies, *Butterfield 8* (1960), and *Who's Afraid of Virginia Wolf?* (1965).
Ellen Burstyn	Academy Award winner, Best Actress, for her role in the movie, *Alice Doesn't Live Here Anymore* (1974).
Elsa	The lioness whose story is told in the movie *Born Free* and in a television series. Elsa's story was first told in a book by Joy Adamson.
Emil Jennings	Academy Award winner, Best Actor, for his role in the movie, *The Way of All Flesh* (1927).
Emma Thompson	Academy Award winner, Best Actress, for her role in the movie, *Howard's End* (1992).
Ernest Borgnine	Academy Award winner, Best Actor, for his role in the movie, *Marty* (1954).

Ernie	One of the muppet characters in the television series *Sesame Street*. (See BERT and OSCAR THE GROUCH.)
Ethel Mertz	The wife of Fred Mertz in the *I Love Lucy* television series.
Ewok	One of the furry, teddy bearlike creatures in the movie *The Return of the Jedi*.
F. Murray Abraham	Academy Award winner, Best Actor, for his role in the movie, *Amadeus* (1984).
Fantasia	A 1940 Walt Disney feature film.
Farrah (Fawcett)	The actress who first became famous in the television series *Charlie's Angels*.
Faye Dunaway	Academy Award winner, Best Actress, for her role in the movie, *Network* (1976).
Felix	The fussy character played by Jack Lemmon in the movie *The Odd Couple* and by Tony Randall in the television series.
Festus	The old deputy in the television series *Gunsmoke*.
Figaro	The kitten who kissed a fish in Walt Disney's animated film, *Pinocchio* (1940).
Flower	The skunk in the animated feature movie *Bambi* (1942).
Fonzie	The nickname of the cool high school dropout, played by Henry Winkler, in the television series *Happy Days*.

Forrest Gump	Title character in the Academy Award-movie staring TOM HANKS.
Frank Sinatra	Academy Award winner, Best Supporting Actor, for his role in the movie, *From Here to Eternity* (1953).
Fredric March	Academy Award winner, Best Actor, for his roles in the movies, *Dr. Jekyll and Mr. Hyde* (1932), and *The Best Years of Our Lives* (1946).
Freeway	The dog in the television series *Hart to Hart.* The Harts found him on the freeway.
Gary Cooper	Academy Award winner, Best Actor, for his roles in the movies, *Sergeant York* (1941), and *High Noon* (1952).
Gene Hackman	Academy Award winner, Best Actor, for his role in the movie, *The French Connection* (1971).
George	Jerry's neurotic friend in the television series *Seinfeld.*
George Arliss	Academy Award winner, Best Actor, for his role in the movie, *Disraeli* (1930).
George Banks	The lead character played by Steve Martin in the movie *Father of the Bride.*
George Burns	A popular comedian (1896–1996); husband of GRACIE ALLEN.
George C. Scott	Academy Award winner, Best Actor, for his role in the movie, *Patton* (1970).
Geraldine Page	Academy Award winner, Best Actress, for her role in the movie, *The Trip to Bountiful* (1985).

Ginger Rogers	Academy Award winner, Best Actress, for her role in the movie, *Kitty Foyle* (1940).
Glenda Jackson	Academy Award winner, Best Actress, for her roles in the movies, *Women in Love* (1970), and *A Touch of Class* (1973).
Glenn Close	Winner of the Tony Award for Best Leading Actress in the musical "Sunset Boulevard;" well-known screen star (*Fatal Attraction*, *The Big Chill*).
Goofy	The not-so-bright, black hound who first appeared in Walt Disney's animated MICKEY MOUSE cartoons.
Goose	The call sign of a pilot in the movie *Top Gun*.
Gordon Gecco	The character played by MICHAEL DOUGLAS in the movie *Wall Street*.
Grace Kelly	Academy Award winner, Best Actress, for her role in the movie, *The Country Girl* (1954).
Gracie Allen	A popular comedienne; wife of GEORGE BURNS.
Greer Garson	Academy Award winner, Best Actress, for the movie, *Mrs. Miniver* (1942).
Gregory Peck	Academy Award winner, Best Actor, for his role in the movie, *To Kill a Mockingbird* (1962).
Grumpy	One of the Seven Dwarfs in Walt Disney's animated movie *Snow White and the Seven Dwarfs* (1937).
Grunt	The dog in the movie *Flashdance*.

Happy	One of the Seven Dwarfs in Walt Disney's animated movie *Snow White and the Seven Dwarfs* (1937).
Hardy (Oliver)	The comedian who co-starred with his partner, LAUREL, in numerous movies.
Harriet (Hilliard Nelson)	The wife of OZZIE in the television series *The Adventures of Ozzie and Harriet* (1952–1966).
Harrison Ford	The actor who played Hans Solo in the *Star Wars* movie series. He also played Indiana Jones in *Raiders of the Lost Ark* and its sequels.
Hawkeye	The irreverent doctor played by Alan Alda in the classic television series *M*A*S*H*.
Hazel (Burke)	The family maid played by Shirley Booth in the television series *Hazel*.
Helen Hayes	Academy Award winner, Best Actress, for her role in the movie, *The Sin of Madelan Claudet* (1931).
Henry Fonda	Academy Award winner, Best Actor, for his role in the movie, *On Golden Pond* (1981).
Herbie	"The Love Bug," a Volkswagen, who is the hero in several movies.
Higgins	The dog in the televison series *Petticoat Junction* (1963–1970). This was movie star BENJI'S first acting role.
Hi-Ho Silver	The LONE RANGER's call to his horse in the television series *The Lone Ranger*.

Holly Hunter	Academy Award winner, Best Actress, for her role in the movie, *The Piano* (1993).
Hooch	The large, ugly mixed-breed dog in the movie *Turner and Hooch* (1989).
Huckleberry Hound	The hero of the first all-animated television series, *Huckleberry Hound,* created by Hanna-Barbera Productions in 1958.
Humphrey Bogart	Academy Award winner, Best Actor, for his role in the movie, *The African Queen* (1951).
Ice Man	The call sign of a pilot played by Val Kilmer in the movie *Top Gun.*
Igor	Dr. Frankenstein's assistant in a series of movies about Frankenstein's monster.
Indiana Jones	The swashbuckling hero of *Raiders of the Lost Ark* (and a series of movies that followed in the 1980s), starring HARRISON FORD.
Ingrid Bergman	Academy Award winner, Best Actress, for her roles in the movies, *Gaslight* (1944), and *Anastasia* (1956).
J. R. (Ewing)	The ruthless Texas oilman in the television series *Dallas.*
Jack Lemmon	Academy Award winner, Best Actor, for his role in the movie, *Save the Tiger* (1973).
Jack Nicholson	Academy Award winner, Best Actor, for his role in the movie, *One Flew Over the Cuckoo's Nest* (1975).
Jackie Gleason	Actor and entertainer best known for his role as RALPH KRAMDEN in the 1950s television series *The Honeymooners.*

James Cagney	Academy Award winner, Best Actor, for his role in the movie, *Yankee Doodle Dandy* (1942).
James Stewart	Academy Award winner, Best Actor, for his role in the movie, *The Philadelphia Story* (1940).
Jane Fonda	Academy Award winner, Best Actress, for her roles in the movies, *Klute* (1971), and *Coming Home* (1978).
Jane Wyman	Academy Award winner, Best Actress, for her role in the movie, *Johnny Belinda* (1948).
Janet Gaynor	Academy Award winner, Best Actress, for her role in the movie, *Seventh Heaven* (1927).
Jay Leno	The host of *The Tonight Show*.
Jedi	A warrior and protector of The Empire in the movies *Star Wars, Return of the Jedi,* and *The Empire Strikes Back*.
Jennifer Jones	Academy Award winner, Best Actress, for her role in the movie, *The Song of Bernadette* (1943).
Jeremy Irons	Academy Award winner, Best Actor, for his role in the movie, *Reversal of Fortune* (1990).
Jerry	The famous mouse who, with his partner, the cat TOM, has appeared in numerous MGM, and later Hanna-Barbera, animated cartoons.
Jessica Lange	Academy Award winner, Best Actress, for her role in the movie, *Blue Sky* (1994).

Jessica Tandy   Academy Award winner, Best Actress, for her role in the movie, *Driving Miss Daisy* (1989).

Jessica   The part played by Angela Lansbury in the popular, long-running television series *Murder She Wrote*.

Jill   TIM'S wife and character in the television series *Home Improvement*.

Joan Crawford   Academy Award winner, Best Actress, for her role in the movie, *Mildred Pierce* (1945).

Joan Fontaine   Academy Award winner, Best Actress, for her role in the movie, *Suspicion* (1941).

Joanne Woodward   Academy Award winner, Best Actress, for her role in the movie, *The Three Faces of Eve* (1957).

Jodie Foster   Academy Award winner, Best Actress, for her roles in the movies, *The Accused* (1988), and *The Silence of the Lambs* (1991).

John Wayne   The famous actor (1907–1979) best known for his portrayals of tough American Western Frontier characters and war heroes. He won an Academy Award in 1969 for *True Grit*.

Jon Voight   Academy Award winner, Best Actor, for his role in the movie, *Coming Home* (1978).

Joker   The sinister character of *Batman* fame played by Cesar Romero in the television series and by Jack Nicholson in the 1989 movie. (See BATMAN.)

Jose Ferrer   Academy Award winner, Best Actor, for his role in the movie, *Cyrano de Bergerac* (1950).

Judy Holliday	Academy Award winner, Best Actress, for her role in the movie, *Born Yesterday* (1950).
Julie Andrews	Academy Award winner, Best Actress, for her role in the movie, *Mary Poppins* (1964).
Julie Christie	Academy Award winner, Best Actress, for her role in the movie, *Darling* (1965).
Katherine Hepburn	Academy Award winner, Best Actress, for her roles in the movies, *Morning Glory* (1932), *Guess Who's Coming to Dinner?* (1967), *The Lion in Winter* (1968), and *On Golden Pond* (1981).
Kathie Lee	Half of the host team of the television talk show *Regis and Kathie Lee.*
Kathy Bates	Academy Award winner, Best Actress, for her role in the movie, *Misery* (1990).
Kimba	The lead character in the 1960s Japanese created television cartoon *Kimba, the White Lion.*
King Kong	Title character of the famous movie about an enormous gorilla (1933).
Kingfish	George Stevens's title on the television series *Amos 'n' Andy.*
Kramer	Jerry's eccentric next-door neighbor in the television series *Seinfeld.*
Kukla, Fran & Ollie	The three puppets from the television show *Kukla, Fran, and Ollie.*
Kunta Kinte	The African man captured by slave traders and shipped to America in the television mini-series *Roots* (1977).

Lady	The pretty female cocker spaniel who charmed TRAMP, a disreputable mutt, in Walt Disney Productions' *Lady and the Tramp*.
Larry	One of the characters in the movies series *The Three Stooges*.
Lassie	The collie heroine of the movie *Lassie Come Home* (1943), based on a novel by Eric Knight. This Lassie, followed by many generations of descendants, starred in seven movie sequels, "The Lassie Radio Show," and the *Lassie* television series.
Laurel (Stan)	The slapstick comedian who co-starred with his partner, HARDY, in numerous movies.
Laurence Olivier	Academy Award winner, Best Actor, for his role in the movie, *Hamlet* (1948).
Laverne	Title character, played by Penny Marshall in the 1970s television series *Laverne and Shirley*.
Lee Marvin	Academy Award winner, Best Actor, for his role in the movie, *Cat Ballou* (1965).
Leo	The Metro-Goldwyn-Mayer (MGM) trademark—a lion that appeared on screen in hundreds of movies.
Lionel Barrymore	Academy Award winner, Best Actor, for his role in the movie, *Free Soul* (1930).
Little Dan	A redbone hunting hound in the novel *Where the Red Fern Grows*.
Little Orphan Annie	The little girl created in a comic strip of the same name by Harold Gray in 1924. Little Orphan Annie has appeared in several movies, the first in 1932.

Liza Minnelli	Academy Award winner, Best Actress, for her role in the movie, *Cabaret* (1972).
Lone Ranger	The masked hero of the television series *The Lone Ranger.*
Loretta Young	Academy Award winner, Best Actress, for her role in the movie, *The Farmer's Daughter* (1947).
Louise Fletcher	Academy Award winner, Best Actress, for her role in the movie, *One Flew Over the Cuckoo's Nest* (1975).
Lucy Ricardo	RICKY RICARDO'S wife and star of the 1950s *I Love Lucy* television series starring Lucille Ball.
Luise Rainer	Academy Award winner, Best Actress, for her role in the movie, *The Good Earth* (1937).
Luke Skywalker	The hero of the movie *Stars Wars* (1977) and its sequels.
MacGyver	The title character of a television series.
Maggie Smith	Academy Award winner, Best Actress, for her role in the movie, *The Prime of Miss Jean Brodie* (1969).
Magnum (Thomas)	The private investigator played by Tom Selleck in the television series *Magnum, P.I.*
Marie Dressler	Academy Award winner, Best Actress, for her role in the movie, *Min and Bill* (1930).
Marilyn Monroe	Famous celebrity and personality known for her blonde hair and voluptuousness.

Marlee Matlin	Academy Award winner, Best Actress, for her role in the movie, *Children of a Lesser God* (1986).
Marlon Brando	Academy Award winner, Best Actor, for his roles in the movies, *On the Waterfront* (1954), and *The Godfather* (1972).
Mary Pickford	Academy Award winner, Best Actress, for her role in the movie, *Coquette* (1928).
Maverick	The pilot call sign of the lead character played by Tom Cruise in the movie *Top Gun*. Also title of a television series starring James Garner.
Maximilian Schell	Academy Award winner, Best Actor, for his role in the movie, *Judgement at Nuremberg* (1961).
Maynard (G. Krebs)	DOBIE GILLIS's beatnik buddy in the television series *The Many Loves of Dobie Gillis*.
McCloud	The cowboy detective in the television series *McCloud*.
Meatball	A mixed-breed dog who appeared in *Black Sheep Squadron*, a television series with Robert Conrad.
Meathead	ARCHIE BUNKER's derogatory name for his son-in-law in the television series *All in the Family*.
Mel Gibson	Actor and star of numerous movies including *Mad Max*, the *Lethal Weapon* series, and *Braveheart*, which he also directed.
Meryl Streep	Academy Award winner, Best Actress, for her role in the movie, *Sophie's Choice* (1982).

Mia (Farrow)	An actress who has appeared in a variety of movies, including several by Woody Allen.
Michael Douglas	Academy Award winner, Best Actor, for his role in the movie, *Wall Street* (1987).
Mickey Mouse	The world famous star of numerous Walt Disney animated cartoons and movies, and of *The Mickey Mouse Club* television show.
Mickey Rooney	The movie actor known for his movies with Judy Garland in the 1930s and '40s, his Andy Hardy movies, and his part in *National Velvet* (1944).
Milo	Title character in the movie *Milo and Otis*.
Minnie Mouse	Animated cartoon star; MICKEY MOUSE'S female counterpart.
Miss Ellie	J. R. EWING'S mother in the television series *Dallas*.
Miss Kitty	The owner of Dodge City's bar in the television series *Gunsmoke*.
Miss Piggy	The outrageous leading lady of television's *The Muppet Show* and of *The Muppet Movie* (1979).
Moe	One of the character in *The Three Stooges*.
Morris	The famous cat that appeared in commercials for 9-Lives Cat Food. Morris also appeared in the movie *Shames* (1972), and in 1973 received the first Patsy Award for an animal in commercials.
Mr. T	The impressively large actor who appeared in the television series *The A-Team* and with SYLVESTER STALLONE in one of the sequels to the movie *Rocky*.

Munchkin	One of a group of little people visited by Dorothy in the cinema classic, *The Wizard of Oz*.
Navin	The character played by Steve Martin in the movie *The Jerk*.
Neil	The alcoholic St. Bernard from the television series *Topper*.
Nina Banks	Played by Diane Keaton, co-star and wife of character George Banks in the movie *Father of the Bride*.
Norma Shearer	Academy Award winner, Best Actress, for her role in the movie, *The Divorce* (1929).
007	The code number for the British spy James Bond, the hero of a series of movies based on novels by Ian Fleming.
Old Dan	A redbone hunting hound from the novel *Where the Red Fern Grows*.
Old Yeller	The rugged, stray yellow-gold dog who was adopted in the movie *Old Yeller*, based on Fred Gipson's book *Old Yeller*. (See also *Old Yeller* in Chapter 10.)
Olivia de Havilland	Academy Award winner, Best Actress, for her roles in the movies, *To Each His Own* (1946), and *The Heiress* (1949).
Omar (Sharif)	The Middle Eastern actor who appeared in numerous movies.
Opie	The boy who portrayed the young son of Andy Griffith in the television series *The Andy Griffith Show*.
Oprah Winfrey	Television talk show hostess and personality.

Screen and Television

Oscar	The sloppy character played by Walter Matthau in the movie *The Odd Couple* and by Jack Klugman in the television series.
Oscar the Grouch	One of the muppet characters in the television series *Sesame Street*. (See BERT and ERNIE.)
Otis	Title character in the movie *Milo and Otis*.
Otto	CHARLIE'S buddy in the 1989 musical cartoon *All Dogs Go To Heaven*.
Ozzie (Nelson)	Main character and husband of HARRIET on the television series *The Adventures of Ozzie and Harriet*.
Patricia Neal	Academy Award winner, Best Actress, for her role in the movie, *Hud* (1963).
Paul Lucas	Academy Award winner, Best Actor, for his role in the movie, *Watch at the Rhine* (1943).
Paul Newman	Academy Award winner, Best Actor, for his role in the movie, *The Color of Money* (1986).
Paul Scofield	Academy Award winner, Best Actor, for his role in the movie, *A Man for All Seasons* (1966).
Pebbles	Fred and Wilma Flintstone's daughter in Hanna-Barbera's animated television cartoon *The Flintstones*.
Pegleg Pete	The villainous bulldog with a wooden leg who appeared with MICKEY MOUSE in the Walt Disney films, *Steamboat Willie* (1928) and *Gallopin' Gaucho* (1929).

Pepe Le Pew	The French skunk who appears in several Warner Brothers' animated cartoons.
Percy	The dog in Disney's animated movie *Pocahontas*.
Pete the Pup	The American pit bull terrier with a black circle around one eye and a patch over the other, who appeared in more than eighty episodes of Hal Roach's *Our Gang* comedies.
Peter Finch	Academy Award winner, Best Actor, for his role in the movie, *Network* (1976).
Peter Pan	The principal character in a play by J. M. Barrie about a boy who didn't want to grow up. Subsequently, he was recreated in the Walt Disney animated movie *Peter Pan*.
Pluto	Walt Disney's lovable animated hound who appears with MICKEY MOUSE in many of his cartoons.
Pocahontas	Title character in Disney's 1995 animated movie about the Native American Indian maiden who fell in love with Captain John Smith.
Popeye	The sailor who derives his strength from eating spinach. Popeye appeared first in comic strips, and later in animated cartoons and movies.
Potsie	Richie Cunningham's friend in the television series *Happy Days*.
Princess Leia	The heroine of the movie *Stars Wars* (1977) and its sequels.
Pyewacket	The cat in the film *Bell, Book, and Candle*.

Quincy	Title character in the television series staring Jack Klugman who played a medical examiner.
Radar	The bespectacled corporal with E.S.P. in the television series *M*A*S*H*.
Ralph Kramden	The high-strung bus driver played by JACKIE GLEASON in the television series *The Honeymooners*.
Rambo	The character played by SYLVESTER STALLONE in the movie *First Blood* and its sequels.
Ray Milland	Academy Award winner, Best Actor, for his role in the movie, *The Lost Weekend* (1945).
Regis	Half of the host team of the television talk show *Regis and Kathie Lee*.
Rex Harrison	Academy Award winner, Best Actor, for his role in the movie, *My Fair Lady* (1964).
Rhubarb	The striped cat who played the lead role in the 1951 movie version of H. Allen Smith's *Rhubarb* (1946). Rhubarb won a Patsy Award for his performance, and then played Minerva in television's *Our Miss Brooks*. In 1962, Rhubarb won another Patsy as Cat in *Breakfast at Tiffany's*.
Richard Dreyfuss	Academy Award winner, Best Actor, for his role in the movie, *The Golden Girl* (1977).
Ricky Ricardo	Lucy's husband and band leader played by Desi Arnaz in the popular television series *I Love Lucy*.

Rin Tin Tin	The German shepherd who after his first film, *Where the North Begins* (1923), appeared in more than forty movies in nine years. His offspring, all given the same name, appeared in subsequent movies and in the television series, *The Adventures of Rin Tin Tin*.
Robert De Niro	Academy Award winner, Best Actor, for his role in the movie, *Raging Bull* (1980).
Robert Donat	Academy Award winner, Best Actor, for his role in the movie, *Goodbye Mr. Chips* (1939).
Robert Duvall	Academy Award winner, Best Actor, for his role in the movie, *Tender Mercies* (1983).
Robin	The younger half of the BATMAN and Robin combination known as "The Dynamic Duo."
Rochester (Van Jones)	Jack Benny's valet, played by Eddie Anderson.
Rockford	The private detective played by James Garner on the television series *The Rockford Files*.
Rocky	The boxer played by SYLVESTER STALLONE in the movie *Rocky* and its sequels.
Rod Steiger	Academy Award winner, Best Actor, for his role in the movie, *In the Heat of the Night* (1967).
Ronald Colman	Academy Award winner, Best Actor, for his role in the movie, *A Double Life* (1947).

Sally Field	Academy Award winner, Best Actress, for her roles in the movies, *Norma Rae* (1979), and *Places in the Heart* (1984).
Sapphire	The wife of George "Kingfish Stevens" in the television series *Amos 'n' Andy*. (See KINGFISH.)
Scar	Uncle and foe of Simba in the animated movie *The Lion King*.
Scarlett (O'Hara)	The heroine, played by Vivien Leigh, of the classic movie *Gone With the Wind* (1939), based on the book by Margaret Mitchell.
Scraps	The white mongrel with a brown spot over one eye, who costarred with CHARLIE CHAPLIN in *A Dog's Life* (1918). Scraps went on to star in fifty more films.
Seinfeld (Jerry)	Entertainer and star of the popular television series *Seinfeld*.
Sheena	The "Queen of the Jungle" played by Irish McCalla in both the movie and the television series.
Shirley Booth	Academy Award winner, Best Actress, for her role in the movie, *Come Back Little Sheba* (1952).
Shirley MacLaine	Academy Award winner, Best Actress, for her role in the movie, *Terms of Endearment* (1983).
Shirley Temple	The most popular child actress of the 1930s, best remembered for her dimples and blonde curly hair.
Shirley	Title character, played by Cindy Williams in the television series *Laverne and Shirley*.

Shogun   The Japanese warrior in the television movie *Shogun*.

Sidney Poitier   Academy Award winner, Best Actor, for his role in the movie, *Lillies of the Field* (1963).

Simba   The lead character in the 1994 Walt Disney animated movie *The Lion King*.

Simone Signoret   Academy Award winner, Best Actress, for her role in the movie, *Room at the Top* (1959).

Sir Alec Guinness   Academy Award winner, Best Actor, for his role in the movie, *The Bridge Over the River Kwai* (1957).

Sissy Spacek   Academy Award winner, Best Actress, for her role in the movie, *Coal Miner's Daughter* (1980).

Sleepy   One of the Seven Dwarfs in Walt Disney's animated movie *Snow White and the Seven Dwarfs* (1937).

Sly   The nickname for actor SYLVESTER STALLONE.

Sneezy   One of the Seven Dwarfs in Walt Disney's animated movie *Snow White and the Seven Dwarfs* (1937).

Snow White   The fairy tale heroine of Walt Disney's animated movie *Snow White and the Seven Dwarfs* (1937).

Solo   The puniest female pup in an African wild dog pack in Hugo van Lawick's television film *The Wild Dogs of Africa*.

Sophia Loren	Academy Award winner, Best Actress, for her role in the movie, *Two Women* (1961).
Spanky	The fat little boy in the television series *The Little Rascals*.
Spencer Tracy	Academy Award winner, Best Actor, for his roles in the movies, *Captains Courageous* (1937), and *Boys Town* (1938).
Spock	The half Vulcan, half human commander of the *Starship Enterprise* in the television series *Star Trek*.
Spuds Mackenzie	The bull terrier, who was known as the "Party Animal," and advertised Budweiser beer in television commercials.
Squeaky	The little girl in the 1989 animated movie *All Dogs Go To Heaven*.
Striker	The call sign of a pilot in the movie *Top Gun*.
Strongheart	The German shepherd who was the first canine hero of feature films.
Sundance Kid	The western outlaw played by Robert Redford in the 1969 movie *Butch Cassidy and the Sundance Kid*. (See BUTCH CASSIDY.)
Susan Hayward	Academy Award winner, Best Actress, for her role in the movie, *I Want to Live* (1958).
Sylvester	A black-and-white cat who has appeared often with Tweety Pie, the canary, in many Warner Brothers' animated cartoons.
Sylvester Stallone	The actor who has starred in the ROCKY movies and the RAMBO movies.

T. C.	THOMAS MAGNUM'S friend, who pilots a helicopter in the television series *Magnum, P. I.*
Tar Baby	The inanimate baby who mystified all the animals in the Walt Disney movie *Song of the South* (1946); based on Joel Chandler Harris's stories.
Terminator	Title character in a movie series starring Arnold Schwarzenegger.
Thumper	The rabbit in Walt Disney's animated movie *Bambi* (1942). (See BAMBI.)
Tigger	The bouncy tiger in the animated television versions of A. A. Milne's Winnie-the-Pooh stories.
Tim	The star of the television series *Home Improvement.*
Tinkerbell	The tiny fairy in the Walt Disney movie *Peter Pan.*
Toby	KUNTA KINTE'S name as a slave in the television mini-series *Roots* (1977).
Tom Hanks	Academy Award winner, Best Actor, for his roles in the movies, *Philadelphia* (1993), and *Forrest Gump* (1994).
Tom	The famous cat who, with his partner, the mouse JERRY, has appeared in numerous MGM, and later Hanna-Barbera animated cartoons.
Tonto	The LONE RANGER'S Indian companion in both the movie and the television series about *The Lone Ranger.*
Tootsie	The man-turned-woman, played by DUSTIN HOFFMAN in the movie *Tootsie.*

Toto	Dorothy's dog in the movie *The Wizard of Oz* (1939).
Tramp	The stray dog who fell in love with LADY, the pretty cocker spaniel, in Walt Disney Productions' animated feature *Lady and the Tramp*.
Trapper	HAWKEYE's buddy in the television series *M*A*S*H*.
Victor McLaglen	Academy Award winner, Best Actor, for his role in the movie, *The Informer* (1935).
Vivian Leigh	Academy Award winner, Best Actress, for her roles in the movies, *Gone With the Wind* (1939), and *A Streetcar Named Desire* (1951).
Wallace Beery	Academy Award winner, Best Actor, for his role in the movie, *The Champ* (1931).
Wally (Cleaver)	BEAVER's older brother in the television series *Leave It to Beaver*.
Warner Baxter	Academy Award winner, Best Actor, for his role in the movie, *In Old Arizona* (1928)
Wile E. Coyote	The hapless pursuer of Road Runner in a series of animated films.
William Hurt	Academy Award winner, Best Actor, for his role in the movie, *Kiss of the Spider Woman* (1985).
Wilson	TIM and JILL'S next door neighbor in the television series *Home Improvement*.
Wonder Woman	Title character of the superhero played by Linda Carter in the 1970s television series based on the comic book heroine of the 1940s.

Yoda

LUKE SKYWALKER'S mentor who trains Luke to become a JEDI in the movies *The Empire Strikes Back* and *Return of the Jedi*.

Yogi (Bear)

The hero of the animated television cartoon *Yogi Bear,* who lives in Jellystone National Park.

Yukon King

The husky who aided Sergeant Preston of the Northwest Mounted Police in his television show, *Sergeant Preston of the Yukon.*

Yul Brynner

Academy Award winner, Best Actor, for his role in the movie, *The King and I* (1956).

Zeus

One of the two Doberman pinschers owned by Robbin Masters on the television series *Magnum P.I.* (See APOLLO.)

CHAPTER 12

Locations and Places

You don't know what a country we have got till you start prowling around it. Personally, I like the small places and sparsely populated states.

Will Rogers

If you're caught without a map or atlas, herein you'll find that little spot you've been looking for. Or, pick your favorite place as your pet's name. Be creative; be original; be anything or anywhere, but don't let your pet be without a name.

Locations and Places

Acapulco (Mexico)

Africa

Alamo (Texas)

Albany

Amazon (a river in South America)

America

Angola

Asia

Aspen (Colorado)

Austin (Texas)

Azores

Bahamas

Bali

Baltic

Bangkok (Thailand)

Bangladesh

Barbados

Bayou (a marshy creek)

Beijing (China)

Belgium

Belize

Bermuda

Bogota (Colombia)

Bombay

Boston

Brazil

Brazos (a river in Texas)

Broadway (the "Great White Way" in New York City)

Brooklyn (New York)

Burma

Butte (Montana)

Cairo (Eygpt)

Calgary (Canada)

Camelot (the legendary capital of Arthur's kingdom)

Cancun (Mexico)

Carmel (California)

Carolina

Caymen (Islands)

Chad

Chelsea (a district in London and in New York City)

Cheyenne (Wyoming)

Chile

China

Colorado (Rado)

Congo

Cozumel (Mexico)

D. C. (Washington, District of Columbia)

Dakota

Dallas (Texas)

Delaware (Dele)

Denmark

Dixie (a traditional name for the South)

Downtown

Egypt

El Dorado (the legendary City of Gold of the
Spanish explorers)

Fargo (North Dakota)

Fiji

Florida

France

Freeway (a limited-access highway)

Fresno (California)

Gabon

Geneva

Georgia

Ghana

Granada

Greece

Guinea

Guyana

Hawaii

Hilton (a hotel chain)

Holland (The Netherlands)

Houston

Hyatt (a hotel chain)

India

Ixtapa (Mexico)

Jakarta

Jamaica

Jordan

Juneau (Alaska)

Junk Yard Cat

Junk Yard Dog

K. C. (Kansas City, Kansas and Missouri)

Katamandu (Nepal)

Kaunai

Kenya

Keys (a chain of islands off the southern tip of
Florida)

Klondike

Kong (Hong Kong)

L. A. (Los Angeles, California)

Laos

Libya

Loch Ness (Scotland)

Madison

Madrid (Spain)

Mali

Malta

Manzanillo (Mexico)

Marriott (a hotel chain)

Maui

Mazatlan (Mexico)

Memphis (Tennessee)

Monaco

Montana

Morocco

Nassau

Nepal

Nevada

Nieman Marcus (an upscale department store)

Niger

Nile (a river in East Africa)

Oahu

Oman

Osaka

Oslo (Norway)

P.V. (Puerto Vallarta, Mexico)

Palau

Panama

Paris

Pecos (Texas)

Peking (China)

Persia

Peru

Phoenix (Arizona)

Pompeii

Rado (Colorado)

Randolph

Reno

Reykjavik (Iceland)

Rio (Rio de Janeiro, Brazil)

Ritz (a luxury hotel)

Samoa

Seoul

Shade

Shiloh (the name for cities in Tennessee and Jerusalem)

Siam

Sidney (Australia)

Sierra

Spain

Sudan

Tahiti

Taipei

Taj Mahal (an Islamic monument built in India in the seventeenth century)

Tara (a village in Ireland)

Texas (Tex)

Tianjin

Tibet

Timbuktu (a city in Mali)

Locations and Places

Togo (an African nation)
Tonga
Touraine (France)
Tripoli (Libya)
Troy (New York)
Tulsa
Turkey
Tuvalu
Uganda
Utah

Vegas (Las Vegas, Nevada)
Venice (Italy)
Virginia
Waco (Texas)
Wales
Yemen
Yukon
Yuma (Arizona)
Zaire
Zambia

"Brooklyn"

"Fraidy"

CHAPTER 13

Unusual Names and Nicknames

> *. . . people select names for some private reason or for no reason*
> *at all—except to arouse a visitor's curiosity, so that he will exclaim,*
> *"Why in the world do you call your dog that?" The cryptic name*
> *their dogs October, Bennet's Aunt, Three Fifteen, Doc Knows,*
> *Tuesday, Home Fried, Opus 38, Ask Leslie, and Thanks for the*
> *Home Run, Emil. I make it a point simply to pat these unfortunate*
> *dogs on the head, ask no questions of their owners, and go about my*
> *business.*
>
> James Thurber
> from *How to Name a Dog*

One of my clients once told me she had considered renaming her dog after she had to stand in her front yard at midnight calling "Woogie, here Woogie."

But if you're not likely to be concerned with what other people think, be as outrageous as your imagination will allow.

Unusual Names and Nicknames

A. J.
Ace
Al Fresco
Al Poochino
Alfie
Alley Cat
Allie
Alpha
Animal
Apache
April
Arlee
Aztec
B. B.
B. J.
Babbs
Bad Debt
Bandi
Bark-ley
Barks A Lot
Bartholo-mew
Beau Beau
Beaux
Bebe
Bee
Belle

Beta
Bif
Big Boss
Big Boy
Big Daddy
Big Foot
Big Guy
Big John
Big Red
Big'un
Bigbird
Bigun
Billy Bob
Bingo
Binky
Blaze
Bliss
Blitz
Blood
Blowout
Blue
Bo
Bobbi
Bobby
Bobo
Bomber

Boo
BooBoo
Boogie
Boogie Boy
Booh
Booker
Boomer
Boots
Bootsie
Boozer
Bowser
Boy
Boy Dog
Boz
Bozo
Bravo
Briana
Bro
Bubah
Bubba
Bubbles
Buck
Buckaroo
Bucko
Buckshot
Bud

Buddy
Buddyweiser
Buffer
Buffin
Buffy
Bugsy
Bullet
Bun Bun
Buster
Buster Black
Butch
Butterfingers
Butthead
Button(s)
Buzz
Ca Cee
Cadi
Cai
Cali
Calley
Callie
Cally
Candi
Capoochino
Cappy
Caprice

Captain Happy	Chelsea	Cisco	Dagney
Career Girl	Chelsey	Clawdius	Dahli
Cat #1	Chelsia	Clazy	Dar
Cat #2	Chelsie	Club	Dawg
Cat Astrophe	Cheri	Co Co	Dax
Cati	Cherokee	Coco	Daze
Catpuccino	Chew-chee	Coco Bear	Deli
Catrinka	Chickie	Codie	Destiny
Catsanova	Chicle	Cody	Dexter
Catty Wompus	Chief	Collie	Dingbat
Cee Gee	Chilla	Comanche	Dobie
Chainsaw	Chimpy	Cooler	Dobie Won Kanobi
Chamois	Chris	Corker	Donation
Chance	Chrisitiana	Corky	Doo Dah
Chancy	Chrissy	Cotton	Doodle
Chap	Christabel	Cottontail	Doodles
Chapin	Christmas	Cowboy	Doogie Bowser
Chappy	Chu Chen	Crash	Doozie
Chaps	Chu Chu	Cricket	Dough Boy
Charlette	Chuckles	Critter	Doxy
Charley	Chula	Crockett Cat	Dude
Charli	Chump	Crystal	Dudette
Charlie	Chuska	Cuki	Dudlee
Charmin	Cici	D. D.	Duffie
Cheebe	Cinder	D. C.	Duffy
Cheers	Cio Cio Sam	Daffy	Duster

Dusty	Ged	Hojo	Justa Dog
Dutch	Ghillie	Holly Hobbles	K. C.
Dweebe	Gi Gi	Hooter	K. D.
Dy	Gink	Howie	K. J.
Elkie	Girl	Iggy	Kadee
Esti	Girl Dog	Ima Cat	Kali
Eulika	Gizmo	Inca	Kally
Ewoke	Goober	J. D.	Kat
Exxene	Goofie Bear	J. J.	Kater
Farkle	Gorbe Chow	Jammer	Keba
Fella	Grammar	Jasmine	Keesha
Ferret Fawcett	Gringo	Jenn-i-purr	Keeta
Fifi	Grommet	Jetta	Kelli
Fila	Groove Dog	Jillsy	Kevin Bacon
Flakes	Groovey	Jimbo	Key Key
Flaps	Grrrr	Jingles	Keys
Flower	H. T.	Jinx	Kiki
Fluffer	Hailey	Jip	Kinki
Fluffles	Half Pint	Jo Jo	Kit Kat
Flush	Hamlet	Joker	Kitsy
Fragment	Hawg	Jossie	Kitt
Fraidy	Hazard	Jr.	Kittens
Freebee	Hef	Jukie	Kitter
Friday	Hekter	Jumbo	Kitti
Fusby	Helen Dalmation	Just A Minute	Kitty Boy
G'Day	Hi Pockets	Justa Cat	Kitty Carlyle

Kitty Q	Lou Lou	Miffy	Molley
Kitty Tom	Lutino	Milo	Moma
Knuckles	Mac Duff	Mimi	Momma Dog (Cat)
Kobi	Mackie	Mimie	Moo Moo
Kodak	Maddie	Minnesota Cats	Mopsy
Kokomo	Mail	Minni	Mortikie
Kringles	Majic	Minnie	Morty
Kristil	Mama Trouble	Minnie Paws	Moss
Kuchen	Mao Tse Tongue	Miss Behavin'	Mouse Tse Tung
Kwik	Mary Dog	Miss Chevious	Mr. Cuddles
Kyrie	Mate	Miss Fortune	Mr. Kitty
Lace	Maudie	Miss Kitty	Mr. Stubbs
Lacey	Maverick	Miss Take	Mr. T
Lady Gal	Maxi	Miss Tickle	Mrs. T
Lady Lin	Mc Gruffen	Missy	Ms. Muffet
Lexie	Me Too	Misty	Mudd
Li'l Guy	Meathead	Mitch	Muff
Li'l Honeysuckle	Meetsie	Mitzi	Muffer
Lia	Meow	Mitzie	Muffett
Liberce	Meow Say Tongue	Mitzu	Muffie
Little B	Mercy	Mixture	Muffy
Little Bit	Merry Christmas	Mo	Muggs
Little Girl	Mew	Mo Jo	Mugsie
Little Kitty	Mew Mew	Moe	Munchkin
Lobo	Mia Ferret	Moffie	Musgly
Lolo	Middie	Mofford	Mutzie

Unusual Names and Nicknames

Navajo	Penny	Pozzo	R. B.
New Kitty	Peppy	Princess Daisy	Rags
Nic Nac	Perky	Princess Josette	Rainbow
Nicky	Petunia	Princess Tiffany	Ralfy
Niki	Phideaux	Priss	Rascal
Nikke	PiCatSo	Prissy	Rasta
No White	Pinky	Pudder	Rat
Nooner	Pitney	Puffy	Ratus
Odd Ball	Podnah	Pugsly	Raven
Oh No	Pojoo	Punkie	Razz
Okie	Polecat	Punky	Razzy
Ombre	Poli	Pup	Red Neck
Owlpuccino	Polson	Pupdog	Reggie
P. B.	Ponch	Pupper	Remington
P. C.	Poo Bee Bear	Puppy	Ringo
P. C. Jr.	Pooch	Pups	Rinky Dink
P. J.	Poochie	Pupster	Rip
Pandy	Poochkie	Pupus	Rip Van Beagle
Papito	Pooh	Purr	Rockey
Papoose	Pooh Bear	Purr Son	Rodeo
Paraphernalia (Pari)	Pooky	Purrbert	Rolf
Paw Pet	Pooper	Purrsilla	Rollie
Peace	Poops	Purrsnickitty	Romer
Pebbles	Pooter	Puss	Roo
Pee Dee	Poppy	Puss Cat	Rosco
Pennie	Potsi	Pussy	Roscoe

Rose	Sarg	Sebo	Shorty Bob
Rosebud	Sashi	Seminole	Shotie
Rosie	Sassy	Shadie	Shu Shu
Roxie	Sassy San	Shady	Si
Roxy	Saturday	Shammy	Siah
Ruffles	Saucer	Sheba	Silver Bell
S. L. O'Pokey	Sawdust	Sheeba	Sioux
Saige	Scamp	Shimmy	Sir Chadwick
Saint Bernie Nard	Scat Cat	Shinola	Sir Woody
Samba (o)	Schwatz	Shoebutton	Sissie
Sami	Scottie	Shooter	Sissy

"Splash"

Sister	Sophistocat	Stickers	Tasi
Skeeter	SoSueMe	Stinker	Taski
Skinner	Spade	Stormy	Tatters
Skipper	Sparky	Striker	Tattoo
Skippy	Special	Strubie	Tawnya
Skitter	Speckles	Stud	Taz
Skitty	Spike	Stymie	Ted E. Bear
Skunky	Spiker	Su-Lin	Tennie
Skwiggles	Spikey	Sue E.	Tex
Slick	Splash	Suki	Thomas Our Cat
Slugger	Split	Sundance	Thunder
Smitty	Spooner	Sunday	Tic Tac
Snapper de Aire	Sport	Sunnie	Tick Tock
Snert	Spring	Sunny	Ticker
Snoobie	Sprinkle	Sunny Cat	Tidbit
Snooker	Spunky	Sunspot	Tiffy
Snooky	Squeaker	Supplies	Tikki
Snoops	Squeakers	Suzie Queen	Tiko
Snow Bear	Squealer	T. C.	Timex
Snowball	Squish	T. J.	Tinker
Snubbs	Star	Taboo	Tippy
Snuff	Stardust	Taffi	Tipster
Sonny	Starr	TAG Heuer	Tipsy
Soo	Stash	Tai	Tobe
Soo Shi	Static	Tally	Tobi
Sooka	Sterling	Tashi	Tobia

Toddy
Tomahawk
Toodles
Toot
Toot Toot
Tootie
Tootsie
Topper
Torti
Tortilla
Trapper
Trendsetter
Trixie

Trooper
Trouffels
Tuffy
Turbo
Turkey
Tusche
Twerp
Twinkle Toes
Twit
Uga
Velcro
Wagley
Waterford

Weebles
Wetta
Whacker
Whiplash
Whisper
Whiz Bang
Whiz O
Why Not
Wicket
Wifferdill
Wild Child
Wild Thing
Wildfire

Willow
Wimpy
Winkie
Wisky Blue
Wizard
Woogy
Woopsie
Wova
YoYo
Zac
Zee
Zero
Zip

CHAPTER 14

Cartoon Characters

Peanuts characters © copyright 1950, 1952, 1958 by United Features Syndicate.

Charles Schultz
from *You Don't Look 35, Charlie Brown*

Your pet may be the perfect Daffy Duck or Roadrunner—guaranteed to make you laugh. But plan ahead! When he or she is testing your patience, a stern "Jughead, I told you to behave" may change your stern countenance into a smiling face.

Cartoon Characters

Al Capp	Cartoonist; creator of "Lil' Abner."
Albert	A main character in "Pogo."
Alley Oop	Title character.
Alvin	A character in *The Chipmunks*.
Andy Capp	Title character.
Angelica Pickles	Character in *Rugrats*.
Animal Crackers	Title character.
Annie (Little Orphan)	Title character.
Archie	Title character.
B. C.	Title character.
Bam Bam	A character in *The Flintstones*.
Barney Google	Title character.
Barney Rubble	A character in *The Flintstones*.
Bart Simpson	Character in *The Simpsons*.
Batman	Title character.

Beetle Bailey	Title character.
Beauregard Bugleboy	A character in "POGO."
Betty	A character in *The Flintstones*.
Betty Boop	Title character.
Bevis	Title character in *Bevis and Butthead*.
Blondie	Title character.
Bluto	Character in *Popeye*.
Bonzo	Title character.
Boris	Character in *Rocky and Bullwinkle*.
Brainey	A character in *The Smurfs*.
Brutus	A villain in *Popeye*.
Bugs Bunny	Title character.
Bullwinkle Moose	Title character in *Rocky and Bullwinkle*.
Bumstead	DAGWOOD and BLONDIE'S family name.
Buster Brown	Title character.
Butthead	Title character in *Bevis and Butthead*.

Cartoon Characters

Buzz Sawyer	Title character.
Calvin	Title character in "Calvin and Hobbes."
Cap Stubbs	Title character.
Captain Marvel	Title character.
Casper	Title character: *Casper the Friendly Ghost.*
Cathy	Title character.
Charlie Brown	Co-star of comic strip and television series "Peanuts."
Chip	Title character in *Chip and Dale.*
Chipmunk(s)	Title character(s).
Chucky Finster	Character in *Rugrats.*
Daffy Duck	Title character.
Dagwood	BLONDIE'S husband.
Daisy	DONALD DUCK'S girlfriend.
Daisy Mae	LIL' ABNER'S girlfriend.
Dale	Title character in *Chip and Dale.*
Dennis the Menace	Title character.
Deputy Dawg	Title character.

Dewey	Character in "Donald Duck."
Dick Tracy	Title character.
Dilbert	Title character.
Dinny	ALLEY OOP's pet dinosaur.
Donald Duck	Title character; also MICKEY MOUSE'S friend.
Doonesbury	Title of strip.
Doug	Title character
Droopy	Title character.
Elmer Fudd	A character in *Looney Tunes*.
Elwood	Title character.
Farley	Dog in the comic strip "For Better or Worse."
Fearless Fosdick	Character in "Lil' Abner."
Felix the Cat	Title character.
Flash Gordon	Title character.
Flintstone(s)	Title character(s).
Fred Basset	Title character.
Fred	Title character in *The Flintstones*.

Cartoon Characters

Fritz	A character in "The Katzenjammer Kids."
Fritz the Cat	Title character.
Garfield	Title character.
Gertie	Title character in "Gertie, the Trained Dinosaur."
Goofy	A character in "Mickey Mouse."
Gordo	Title character.
Grammy	Title character.
Gumby	Title character in *Gumby and Pokey*.
Gummi Bear	Title character.
Hagar the Horrible	Title character.
Hans	A character in "The Katzenjammer Kids."
Happy Hooligan	Title character.
Hazel	Title character.
Heathcliff	Title character.
Heckle and Jeckle	Title characters.
Heifer	Character in *Rocko's Modern Life*.

Henry	Title character.
Hi	Title character of "Hi and Lois."
Hobbes	Title character in "Calvin and Hobbes."
Homer Simpson	Character in *The Simpsons.*
Huckleberry Hound	Title character.
Huey	Character in "Donald Duck."
Ickus	Character in *Real Monsters.*
Ignatz Mouse	Title character.
Jeff	Title character in "Mutt and Jeff."
Jerry	Title character in *Tom and Jerry.*
Jiggs	A character in the cartoon strip "Bringing Up Father."
Joe Cool	SNOOPY's alter ego in "Peanuts."
Joe Palooka	Title character.
Jughead	A character in "Archie."
Jungle Jim	Title character.
Katzenjammer Kids	Title character(s).

Cartoon Characters

Krazy Kat	Title character.
Krumb	Character in *Real Monsters*.
Li'l Abner	Title character.
Lil	Character in *Rugrats*.
Linus	A character in comic strip and television series "Peanuts."
Lisa Simpson	Character in *The Simpsons*.
Little Abner	Title character.
Little Lulu	Title character.
Lois	Title character in "Hi and Lois."
Louie	Character in "Donald Duck."
Luann	Title character.
Lucy	A character in "Peanuts."
Maggie	A character in "Bringing Up Father."
Margaret	A character in "Dennis the Menace."
Marge Simpson	Character in *The Simpsons*.
Marmaduke	Title character.

Maw	A character in "Snuffy Smith."
Mickey Mouse	Title character.
Mighty Mouse	Title character.
Minnie Mouse	MICKEY MOUSE'S girlfriend.
Moon Mullins	Title character.
Mr. Boffo	Title character.
Mr. Dink	Character in *Doug*.
Mr. Magoo	Title character.
Muddy the Mudskipper	Character in *Ren and Stimpy*.
Mutt	Title character in "Mutt and Jeff."
Nancy	Title character.
Napoleon	Title character.
Natasha	Character in *Rocky and Bullwinkle*.
Nermal	Cat in "Garfield" comics.
Nervy Nat	Title character.
Nudnik	Title character.

Oblina	Character in *Real Monsters*.
Odie	GARFIELD's canine friend.
Offisa Bull Pupp	A character in *Krazy Kat*.
Okefenokee	The setting (a swamp) in the series "Pogo."
Olive Oil	POPEYE's girlfriend.
Opus	The penguin in the comic strip series "Bloom County."
Pasquale	Baby boy in the comic strip "Rose is Rose."
Peanuts	Title of comic strip and television series.
Pebbles	A character in the comic strip and television series *The Flintstones*.
Pepe Le Pew	A character in *Looney Tunes*.
Pepe Le Pu	Title character.
Peppermint Patty	A character in the comic strip and television series "Peanuts."
Petunia Pig	A character in "Porky Pig."
Phil	Character in *Rugrats*.
Philbert	Character in *Rocko's Modern Life*.
Phineas T. Bridgeport	A character in "Pogo."

Pig-Pen	A character in the comic strip and television series "Peanuts."
Pink Panther	Title character.
Pluto	MICKEY MOUSE'S dog.
Pogo	Title character.
Pokey	Title character in *Gumby and Pokey.*
Popeye	Title character.
Porkchop	Character in *Doug.*
Porky Pig	Title character.
Prince Valiant	Title character.
Quincy	The iguana in the comic strip "Fox Trot."
Ready	Title character in "Ruff and Ready."
Ren	Title character in *Ren and Stimpy.*
Road Runner	Title character.
Rocko	Title character in *Rocko's Modern Life.*
Rocky (the Flying Squirrel)	Title character in *Rocky and Bullwinkle.*
Rose	Title character in "Rose is Rose."

Cartoon Characters

Ruff	A character in "Dennis the Menace."
Ruff	Title character in "Ruff and Ready."
Sally	A character in the comic strip and television series "PEANUTS."
Schroeder	A character in the comic strip and television series "PEANUTS."
Scooby Doo	Title character.
Simon	Title character: *The Chipmunks.*
Simple J. Malarkey	A character in "Pogo."
Sluggo	(1) Sarge's dog in the comic strip "Beetle Bailey." (2) NANCY'S friend in "Nancy."
Smithers	Character in *The Simpsons.*
Smurf	Title character.
Smurfette	A character in *The Smurfs.*
Snoopy	Title character in the comic strip and television series "Peanuts."
Snuffy Smith	Title character.
Solomon	Title character.
Space Ghost	Title character.
Speedy Gonzales	Title character.

Spike	A character in *Tom and Jerry*.
Spike	Character in *Rugrats*.
Steve Canyon	Title character.
Stimpy	Title character in *Ren and Stimpy*.
Stinky	Character in *Doug*.
Susie	Character in *Rugrats*.
Sweet Pea	Character in "Popeye."
Sylvester	Title character.
Sylvia	Title character.
Tarzan	Title character.
Tintin	Title character.
Tippie	Title character in a comic strip no longer in print.
Tom	Title character in *Tom and Jerry*.
Tommy Pickles	Character in *Rugrats*.
Trudy	Title character.
Tweetie Pie	A character in the comic strip and animated cartoon "Sylvester the Cat."

Cartoon Characters

Veronica	A character in "Archie."
Wile E. Coyote	A character in the comic strip and animated cartoon *The Road Runner*.
Wiley Catt	A character in "Pogo."
Wilma	A character in the comic strip and television series *The Flintstones*.
Wimpie	A character in the comic strip and animated cartoon *Popeye*.
Winnie-the-Pooh	Title character.
Wizard of Id	Title character.
Woodstock	A character in the comic strip and television series "Peanuts."
Woody the Woodpecker	Title character.
Yogi	Title character in *Yogi the Bear*.
Zero	A character in "Beetle Bailey."
Ziggy	Title character.

"Primadonna"

CHAPTER 15

Just for Fun

But I tell you, a cat needs a name that's particular,
A name that's peculiar, and more dignified,
Else how can he keep up his tail perpendicular,
Or spread out his whiskers, or cherish his pride?

T. S. Eliot
from *Old Possum's Book of Practical Cats*

A school mascot or the name of a singer may become your new pet's name. Use this short chapter to give you some ideas; there are only a few names suggested here to get you started on your own list.

ASSORTED NAMES

Ace	Cribbage	Jive	Rock-ola
Baccarat	Cue Ball	Joker	Sailor
Backgammon	D. J.	Keno	Scrabble
Ballerina	Danny Boy	Lawyer	Sergeant Pepper
Banjo	Dealer	Lotto	Shooter
Banker	Diamond	Manager	Slot
Bartender	Dice	Payout	Spade
Bill Bailey	Disco	Pilot	Spin
Blackjack	Doc	Player	Tango
Bluegrass	Floorman	Poker	Tom Dooley
Boogie	Gig 'Em	Primadonna	Trifecta
Card	Gin Rummy	Prof	Trucker
Cha Cha	Jackpot	Purse	Walin' Jennings
Chip	Jazz	Reel	Way Out Willie
Club	Jitter Bug	Rock	Winner

ENTERTAINERS—PAST AND PRESENT

Alan Jackson
Barbara Mandrell
Barbra Streisand
B. B. King
Beatle(s)
Bee Gee(s)
Bette Midler
Bill Cosby
Bill Murray
Billy Joel
Billy Ray Cyrus
Bing Crosby
Blood, Sweat and Tears
Bob Dylan
Bobbie Gentry
Bobby Goldsboro
Bob Hope
Bon Jovi
Bonnie Raitt
Brenda Lee
Bruce Springsteen
Buck Owens
Buddy Hackett

Buddy Holly
Carole King
Charlie Daniels
Charlie Pride
Charlie Rich
Cher
Chet Atkins
Chubby Checker
Chuck Berry
Clint Black
Conway Twitty
Crystal Gayle
Dale Evans
Dan Ayckroyd
David Cooperfield
David Bowie
David Letterman
Dean Martin
Diana Ross
Dolly Parton
Dottie West
Dusty Springfield
Dwight Yoakam
Eagle(s)

Eddie Murphy
Elton John
Elvis Presley
Emmylou Harris
Eric Clapton
Ernest Tubb
Fleetwood Mac
Floyd (Pink Floyd)
Frank Sinatra
Frankie Avalon
Fred Astaire
Gallagher
Garth Brooks
Gene Autry
Gene Kelly
George Burns
George Carlin
George Harrison
George Strait
Gilda Radner
Ginger Rogers
Glen Campbell
Gracie Allen
Groucho Marx

Hank Snow
Hank Williams
Harpo Marx
Harry Chapin
Jack Benny
James Taylor
Jay Leno
Jerry Lewis
Jerry Lee Lewis
Jimmy Buffett
Joan Baez
Joan Rivers
Jimmy Dean
John Denver
Judy Collins
Judy Garland
Julio Iglesias
June Carter
Kenny Rogers
Kris Kristofferson
Lawrence Welk
Lee Greenwood
Lily Tomlin
Linda Ronstadt

Liberace
Lionel Richie
Liza Minnelli
Loretta Lynn
Louis Armstrong
Lyle Lovett
Lynn Anderson
Mac Davis
Madonna
Marie Osmond
Marty Robbins
Mel Tillis
Merle Haggard
Merle Travis
Michael Jackson
Mick Jagger
Milton Berle
Naomi Judd

Natalie Cole
Nat "King" Cole
Neil Sedaka
Olivia Newton-John
Otis Redding
Patsy Cline
Patty Loveless
Paul Anka
Paul Simon
Paul McCartney
Pavarotti
Peter, Paul & Mary
Phil Collins
Randy Travis
Ray Charles
Ray Price
Ray Stevens
Reba McEntire

Red Buttons
Red Skelton
Ricky Van Shelton
Ringo Starr
Rod Stewart
Ronnie Milsap
Roseanne Cash
Roy Acuff
Roy Clark
Roy Orbison
Roy Rogers
Sam Cooke
Sammy Davis Jr.
Selena
Sonny Bono
Steely Dan
Stevie Wonder
Tanya Tucker

Tennessee Ernie Ford
Tex Ritter
Tina Turner
Tom T. Hall
Tony Bennett
Travis Tritt
Trisha Yearwood
U2
Van Halen
Vince Gill
Wayne Newton
Whitney Houston
Willie Nelson
Wynonna Judd

COMPOSERS

Andrew Lloyd Webber	British composer (b. 1948).
Bach	German composer (1685–1750).
Beethoven	German composer (1770–1827)
Cole Porter	American composer (1893–1964).
George Gershwin	American composer (1898–1937).
Irving Berlin	American composer (1888–1989).
Mozart	Austrian composer (1756–1791).
Noel Coward	British composer (1899–1973).

SCHOOL AND COLLEGE MASCOTS AND NICKNAMES

Aggie	Devil	Pacer	Sooner
Bevo	Gator	Panther	Spartan
Big Al	Grizzly	Racer	Titan
Bomber	Hoosier	Rambler	Trojan
Blazer	Horned Toad	Razorback	Viking
Bruin	Husky	Red Raider	Wahoo
Cadet	Ichabod	Rocket	
Charger	Nittany Lion	Reville	
Demon	Jasper	Seminole	

"Peter, Paul & Mary"

"Slam Dunk"

CHAPTER 16

Sports

The game ain't over till it's over.

Yogi (Lawrence Peter) Berra

Throughout the past century, sports has played a big part in our lives. Whether you are an avid sports buff or a part-time fan keeping up with your favorite team, consider some of these entries in your selection of your pet's name.

A. J. Foyt	A famous race car driver; four-time Indy 500 winner.
Ace	In tennis, an unreturnable serve.
Adidas	A brand of athletic wear.
Al Unser	Auto Racing: One of IndyCar's top twenty drivers.
Al Worthington	Baseball: A pitcher for the Giants in the 50s and the Twins and the White Sox in the 60s.
Amy Alcott	Golf: 1980 U.S. Women's Open Champion.
Andre Ware	Football: 1989 winner of the Heisman Memorial Trophy.
Annika Sorenstam	Golf: Winner of the 1995 U.S. Women's Open.
Archie Griffin	Football: 1974 and 1975 winner of the Heisman Memorial Trophy (Ohio State University).
Arnold Palmer	Golf: Winner of four Masters Tournaments, one U.S. Open, and two British Open Tournaments.
Babe Ruth	Baseball: One of the most famous all-time athletes, Ruth hit sixty home runs in 1927 while playing for the New York Yankees.
Balk	In baseball, an incomplete or misleading motion.
Barry Sanders	Football: 1988 winner of the Heisman Memorial Trophy (Oklahoma State University).

Bart Starr	Football: Hall of Famer; active 1965 to 1973; associated mainly with the Chicago Bears.
Batter	In baseball, the player attempting to hit the ball.
Bear Bryant	Football: Coach at Texas A & M University in the 50s and at the University of Alabama in the 60s, 70s, and 80s.
Ben Hogan	Golf: Winner of four U.S. Opens. In 1953, he won the Masters, the U.S. Open, and the British Open.
Betsy King	Golf: Winner of the 1989 and 1990 U.S. Women's Open.
Billy Jean King	Tennis: Winner of several indoor, U.S. Open, and Wimbledon titles (among others) during the 1960s and 1970s.
Billy Sims	Football: 1978 winner of the Heisman Memorial Trophy.
Birdie	In golf, a score of one under PAR.
Bo Jackson	Football: 1985 Heisman Memorial Trophy winner (Auburn University).
Bob Cousy	Basketball: A Boston Celtics standout, Cousy scored fifty points in a 1953 playoff game—a record at the time.
Bobby Hull	Ice Hockey: Player, elected to the Hall of Fame, having spent the most productive years with the Chicago Black Hawks.
Bobby Mitchell	Football: First black player to be a member of the Washington Redskins; he was later elected to the Hall of Fame.
Bobby Unser	Auto Racing: One of IndyCar's top twenty drivers.

Bogey	In golf, a score of one over PAR.
Boog Powell	Baseball: Outfielder for the Baltimore Orioles in the 60s and 70s; best known for his appearance on Miller Lite beer commercials.
Boris Becker	Tennis: Three-time winner of Wimbledon (1985, 1986, and 1989) and winner of the U.S. Open (1989).
Boxer	In boxing, one who fights with his fists.
Bunker	In golf, a sand TRAP.
Cal Ripkin	Baseball: On September 6, 1995, broke Lou Gehrig's record of 2130 for most consecutive games played.
Carl Lewis	Track and Field: World record holder in the 100-Meter Dash and the 200-Meter Dash (1984 Summer Olympic Games).
Casey Stengel	Baseball: Former manager of the New York Yankees; led his team to ten American League pennant titles from 1949 to 1980.
Cassius Clay	See MUHAMMAD ALI.
Catcher	In baseball, the player who receives the pitches from the PITCHER.
Center	In football, the player who hands the ball to the QUARTERBACK.
Charles White	Football: 1979 winner of the Heisman Memorial Trophy (USC).
Charley Taylor	Football: A receiver for the Washington Redskins who caught a record 649 passes from 1964 to 1977.

Charlie Ward	Football: 1993 winner of the Heisman Memorial Trophy (Florida State University).
Chris Evert	Tennis: Winner of several indoor, U.S. Open, and Wimbledon titles (among others) during the 1970s and 1980s.
Dan Marino	Football: Leader in passing in the NFL.
David Robinson	Basketball: NBA Rookie of the Year in 1989–1990 (San Antonio Spurs); 1991 rebound leader.
Desmond Howard	Football: 1991 winner of the Heisman Memorial Trophy (Michigan).
Dick Butkus	Football: Hall of Famer; active 1965 to 1973; associated mainly with Chicago Bears.
Dizzy Dean	Baseball: Winner of National League's Most Valuable Player Award, 1934.
Doug Flutie	Football: 1984 Heisman Memorial Trophy winner (Boston College).
Dribble	In basketball, bouncing the ball on the floor.
Driver	In golf, the club normally used on the tee box for attaining distance.
Eagle	In golf, a score of two under PAR.
Earl Campbell	Football: 1977 Heisman Memorial Trophy winner (University of Texas).
Eddie George	Football: 1995 winner of the Heisman Memorial Trophy.
Ernie Banks	Baseball: Hit 512 National League home runs.

Evonne Goolagong   Tennis: Winner at Wimbledon in 1971 and 1980.

Extra Point   In football, scoring a point after a TOUCHDOWN.

Fastball   In baseball, a PITCH thrown at a high rate of speed.

Featherweight   In boxing, a BOXER weighing between 118 and 127 pounds.

Florence Griffith   Track and Field: 1988 Olympic gold medalist.

Floyd Patterson   Boxing: World HEAVYWEIGHT champion, 1956 to 1959, 1960 to 1962.

Fly Ball   In baseball, a pitch that is hit high into the air.

Flyweight   In boxing, a BOXER in the lightest weight class (weighing 112 pounds or less).

Fran Tarkenton   Football: A leading NFL touchdown passer and leader in passing yards.

Frisbee   A brand of toy that resembles a "flying saucer."

Fullback   In football, a player in the BACKFIELD.

Fumble   In football, the act of an offensive ball carrier dropping the ball.

Fuzzy Zoeller   Golf: Winner of the 1979 Masters and the 1984 U.S. Open.

Gary Player   Golf: 1962 and 1972 P.G.A. Champion, winner of the 1965 U.S. Open, the 1961, 1974, and 1978 Masters, and the 1959, 1968, and 1974 British Open.

George Blanda   Football: Long-time NFL leader in points scored.

George Foreman   Boxing: World HEAVYWEIGHT champion, 1970 to 1973.

George Rogers   Football: 1980 winner of the Heisman Memorial Trophy (South Carolina).

Gino Torretta   Football: 1992 winner of the Heisman Memorial Trophy (Miami).

Goal   In ice hockey, the area behind the net through which players try to advance a PUCK. In basketball, the HOOP into which players throw a ball.

Goalie   In ice hockey, the player who defends the GOAL.

Grounder   In baseball, a ball hit on the ground by the BATTER.

Gutter   In bowling, the area on either side of the lane.

Halfback   In football, a player in the BACKFIELD.

Hand-off   In football, one offensive player giving the ball to another offensive player.

Hank Aaron   Baseball: Hall of Famer and holder of the following records: Home runs (1st), Runs scored (2nd), and Hits (3rd).

Hazard   An obstacle on a golf course.

Heavyweight   In boxing, the class of BOXERS in the heaviest weight class, weighing over 175 pounds.

Herschel Walker   Football: 1982 Heisman Memorial Trophy winner (University of Georgia).

Hit-and-Run   In baseball, a play in which the runner progresses to the next base simultaneously with the BATTER hitting the PITCH.

Sports

Hobie Cat	A brand of sailboat.
Hollis Stacy	Golf: 1977 and 1978 U.S. Women's Open champion.
Home Run	In baseball, a play in which the ball hit by the BATTER allows him to proceed around all three bases safely to home plate.
Homer	See HOME RUN.
Hoop	In basketball, the goal.
Interception	In football, a play in which a defensive player catches a pass in the air.
Jack Dempsey	Boxing: World HEAVYWEIGHT champion, 1919 to 1926.
Jack Nicklaus	Golf: Winner of the following tournaments: six Masters, four U.S. Opens, five PGA's, and three British Opens.
Jackie Joyner-Kersee	Track and Field: 1988 Olympic gold medalist.
Jan Stephenson	Golf: 1983 U.S. Women's Open champion.
Jane Geddes	Golf: 1986 U.S. Women's Open champion.
Janet Alex	Golf: 1982 U.S. Women's Open champion.
Jesse Owens	Track and Field: Winner of four Olympic gold medals in 1936.
Jim Brown	Football: Professional football Hall of Famer; Cleveland Browns, 1957 to 1965.

Jim Thorpe	Pentathlon and Decathlon: 1912 Olympics in Stockholm, Sweden.
Joe DiMaggio	Baseball: Former New York Yankees outfielder; hit safely in 50 consecutive baseball games.
Joe Frazier	Boxing: World HEAVYWEIGHT champion, 1970 to 1973.
Joe Louis	Boxing: World HEAVYWEIGHT champion from 1937 to 1950.
Joe Montana	Football: All-time NFL leader in pass efficiency.
Joe Namath	Football: The New York Jets QUARTERBACK and Hall of Famer (1985); led his team to a 16-7 victory over the Baltimore Colts in the 1968 football season Super Bowl.
Johnny Bench	Baseball: Former catcher for the Cincinnati Reds; MVP twice.
Johnny Rutherford	Auto Racing: One of IndyCar's top twenty drivers.
Julius Irving	Basketball: Third lifetime NBA leading scorer (30,026 points through 1988 season).
Jump Shot	In basketball, a play in which the ball is propelled toward the GOAL while the player is airborne.
Kareem Abdul-Jabbar	Basketball: Lew Alcindor; Individual NBA scoring champion 1960 to 1972; Milwaukee Bucks.
Kathy Baker	Golf: 1985 U.S. Women's Open champion.
Kickoff	In football, putting the ball into play by kicking it to the opposing team from a stationary position on the ground.

Knuckleball	In baseball, a pitch thrown by gripping the ball with the knuckles of two or three fingers.
KO (Knockout)	In boxing, defeating an opponent by causing him to fall onto the canvas and remain there for a count of ten.
Larry Bird	Basketball: High-scoring forward of the Boston Celtics; winner of the NBA Most Valuable Player Award, 1984.
Laura Davies	Golf: 1987 U.S. Women's Open champion.
Lauri Merten	Golf: Winner of the 1993 U.S. Women's Open.
Layup	In basketball, a shot made by playing the ball off the backboard from close to the basket, usually after driving in.
Lightweight	In boxing, a BOXER weighing between 127 and 135 pounds.
Lob	In basketball, volleyball, and tennis, a shot that attains greater height than normal.
Lou Gehrig	Baseball: Hall of Famer; active from 1923 to 1939; holder of tenth Highest Runs Scored record.
Magic Johnson	Basketball: Winner of the NBA Most Valuable Player Award, 1987; member of the Los Angeles Lakers.
Marcus Allen	Football: 1981 winner of the Heisman Memorial Trophy (USC).
Mario Andretti	Auto Racing: One of IndyCar's top twenty drivers.

Martina Navratilova	Tennis: Winner of several indoor, U.S. Open and Wimbledon titles during the late 1970s and 1980s.
Maury Wills	Baseball: Los Angeles Dodgers' shortstop who set a record in 1962 by stealing 104 bases.
Meg Mallon	Golf: Winner of the 1991 U.S. Women's Open.
Michael Andretti	Auto Racing: One of IndyCar's top twenty drivers.
Michael Jordan	Basketball: NBA Individual Scoring champion 1986 to 1988 (Chicago Bulls); leader in scoring average.
Michael Spinks	Boxing: World HEAVYWEIGHT champion, 1985 to 1986.
Mickey Mantle	Baseball: New York Yankees outfielder who led the American League in home runs four seasons. During his career with the Yankees from 1952 to 1968, his team won eleven pennants and seven World Championships.
Middleweight	In boxing, a BOXER weighing between 148 and 160 pounds.
Mike Ditka	Football: Coach of the Chicago Bears.
Mike Rozier	Football: 1983 winner of the Heisman Memorial Trophy.
Mike Tyson	Boxing: World HEAVYWEIGHT champion 1987 to 1989.
Monica Seles	Tennis: Winner of the U.S. Open in 1991 and 1992, and the 1993 and 1996 Australian Open.
Moses Malone	Basketball: NBA leader in free throws.

Muhammed Ali	Boxing: World HEAVYWEIGHT champion, 1964 to 1967; 1974 to 1978; and 1978 to 1979.
Nancy Lopez	Golf: LPGA leading money winner in 1978, 1979, and 1985.
Nerf	A brand of toy.
Net	In tennis and volleyball, the barrier of meshwork cord that divides the playing field; also, in basketball, the cord under the rim on the backboard.
Nike	A brand of sportswear/shoes.
Nolan Ryan	Baseball: Record holder for most number of lifetime strikeouts by a pitcher (broke 5,000 mark in 1989).
O. J. Simpson	Football: Winner of the 1968 Heisman Memorial Trophy (USC); The first choice at the 1969 pro football draft in which he was paid $250,000 over four years, the most paid for a running back. He later became a sports commentator for ABC and NBC.
O.B.	"Out of bounds": In football and certain other games, the term applies to a ball out of play.
Olin	A brand of snow ski.
Pancho Gonzales	Tennis: Player who dominated the pro tour from 1953 to 1962.
Par	In golf, the score standard for each of the holes on a golf course.
Pat Bradley	Golf: 1981 U.S. Women's Open champion.
Patty Sheehan	Golf: Winner of the 1992 and 1994 U.S. Women's Open.

Penalty	A loss of advantage enforced on a player or team for infraction of a rule.
Pete Rose	Baseball: Leader in total number of lifetime hits (4,256); played mostly with the Cincinnati Reds; suspended in 1989 for betting on baseball.
Pistol Pete	Basketball: Pete Maravich, holder of two college top Single-Game Scoring records: 1969 (66 points); 1970 (69 points); also leading Individual NBA scorer in 1976 to 1977 (2,273 points).
Pitch	In baseball, the term used for the ball when it is thrown by the PITCHER to the BATTER.
Pitcher	In baseball, one who throws the ball to the BATTER.
Pitchout	In baseball, a PITCH deliberately thrown high and outside making it easy for the CATCHER to retrieve.
Polo	A game played by people on horseback, using a wooden mallet to hit a wooden ball.
Popup	In baseball, a ball hit high into the air by the BATTER.
Puck	In ice hockey, the hard rubber disc used in play instead of a ball.
Punt	In football, a kick in which the ball is kicked when dropped from the hands before it touches the ground.
Putter	In golf, the club used to hit the ball into the cup on the green.
Quarterback	In football, the player who receives the ball from the CENTER, calls the signals, and directs the offensive plays of the team.

Randy Matson	Track and field: The Texas A & M shotputter who broke the world record in 1967; he won an Olympic gold medal the following year.
Rashaan Salaam	Football: 1994 winner of the Heisman Memorial Trophy (Colorado).
Rebound	In basketball, the act of retrieving and recovering the ball after a missed shot.
Recovery	In football, the act of regaining possession of the ball after a fumble.
Red Auerbach	Basketball: Former coach of the Boston Celtics.
Red Grange	Football: Illinois University player in the 1920s; he was known as "The Galloping Ghost."
Reebok	A brand of sportswear/shoes.
Referee (Ref)	The official who enforces the rules in sports games.
Reggie Jackson	Baseball: American League Home Run champion 1973, 1975, and 1980.
Rick Mears	Auto Racing: One of IndyCar's top twenty drivers.
Rocky Marciano	Boxing: World HEAVYWEIGHT champion, 1952 to 1956.
Roger Maris	Baseball: Former New York Yankees player; hit more home runs in one season than any other player in history (sixty-one in 1961).
Rookie	All sports: A player in his or her first year.
Rugby	A British game which has similarities to American football, basketball, soccer, and hockey.

Runner	In baseball, the player who attempts to round the bases; also a person who jogs or runs.
Sacrifice	In baseball, a play in which the BATTER is out but a RUNNER advances to another base.
Safety	In football, the grounding of the ball by the offensive team behind its own goal line; a defensive player farthest from the line of SCRIMMAGE.
Sandy Koufax	Baseball: Los Angeles Dodgers pitcher who won the Cy Young Award in 1963, 1965, and 1966.
Scrimmage	A team's practice session.
Server	In tennis, volleyball and certain other games, the player who brings the ball into play.
Shaquille O'Neal	Basketball: Orlando Magic star who was the 1995 scoring leader.
Shortstop	In baseball, the position between second and third base.
Shotgun	A gun that fires multiple pellets through a smooth bore.
Skeet	A sport in which clay targets are thrown into the air and fired at from eight different stations.
Sky Hook	In basketball, a hook shot that attains more than usual height.
Slam Dunk	In basketball, the maneuver in which a player forces the ball into the net from above the rim.
Slingshot	A Y-shaped instrument with elastic bands attached; used for propelling objects.

Sports

Snap	In football, the handing of the ball to the QUARTERBACK through the legs of the CENTER.
Sonny Liston	Boxing: World HEAVYWEIGHT champion 1962 to 1964.
Spalding	A brand of sporting goods.
Spar	In boxing, going through the motions of boxing.
Spare	In bowling, knocking down all ten pins with two successive rolls of the ball.
Sparky Anderson	Baseball: Manager of the Cinncinati Reds until 1979 at which time he became manager of the Detroit Tigers.
Speedo	Brand of swimwear.
Spoon	Giving the ball an upward movement in certain games.
Stan Musial	Baseball: Player for the St. Louis Cardinals in the 50s and 60s; a Hall of Famer, Musial held National League records for having played more games (3,026) than any other National Leaguer; he also held league records for most runs batted in, most at bats, most runs scored, and most base hits.
Steffi Graf	Tennis: Winner of several U.S. Open, Indoor and Wimbledon titles during the 1980s and 1990s.
Strike	In baseball, a PITCH that the BATTER misses; also, a pitch that crosses without the batter making any attempt to swing.
Swish	In basketball, a shot that passses through the rim without touching it.

T. D. (Touchdown)	See TOUCHDOWN.
T.K.O.	Boxing: Technical knock out. This occurs when a match is ended because one of the boxers is unable to continue fighting, but has not been knocked down and counted out by the referee.
Tackle	In football, stopping another player by seizing him and bringing him to the ground; the players positioned between the guard and the end.
Ted Williams	Baseball: National Hall of Famer; six time American League Batting champion from 1939 to 1960.
Tim Brown	Football: 1987 winner of the Heisman Memorial Trophy (Notre Dame).
Tom Landry	Football: Former coach of the Dallas Cowboys.
Tony Dorsett	Football: 1976 Heisman Memorial Trophy winner.
Touchback	In football, touching the ball to the ground behind one's own goal line, the ball having been impelled over the goal line by an opponent.
Touchdown	In football, scoring six points.
Trap	In golf, an area filled with sand to serve as a HAZARD.
Ty Cobb	Baseball: A Detroit Tigers' player in the early 1900s who had a lifetime batting average of .367 and 4,191 base hits. He was the first member of the National Baseball Hall of Fame.
Ty Detmer	Football: 1990 winner of the Heisman Memorial Trophy (Brigham Young University).

Sports

Umpire (Ump)	A person designated to rule on various plays, especially in baseball.
Vince Lombardi	Football: Hall of Famer; coach of the Green Bay Packers and Washington Redskins from 1959 to 1970.
Vinny Testaverde	Football: 1986 winner of the Heisman Memorial Trophy (Miami).
Volley	In tennis and volleyball, a series of successive returns of the ball from one side to the other.
Walter Payton	Football: All-time NFL leader in rushing yards.
Wedge	In golf, a club with the head positioned at a large angle to allow for loft when the ball is hit.
Welterweight	In boxing, a BOXER who weighs between 136 and 147 pounds.
Whitey Ford	Baseball: New York Yankees pitcher in the 50s and 60s; holder of the following lifetime World Series records: Most Victories (pitcher), Most Innings Pitched, Most Consecutive Scoreless Innings, and Most Strikeouts by Pitcher.
Willie Mays	Baseball: San Francisco Giants and New York Mets outfielder who had a career batting average of .302. His lifetime total of 660 homers was topped only by BABE RUTH and HANK AARON; Hall of Famer.
Wilson	Brand of sports equipment.
Wilt Chamberlain	Basketball: Star of the Philadelphia Warriors and the Los Angeles Lakers, scoring a record 100 points in one game. He averaged 50.4 points per game during the 1961 to 1962 season.

Wimbledon   In tennis, the home (England) of the World Championships since 1908.

Yogi Berra   Baseball: Hall of Famer; active 1946 to 1965. Holder of record number of hits (71) in World Series (lifetime).

"Edsel"

CHAPTER **17**

Transportation

. . . He gives you a wave of his long brown tail
 Which says: "I'll see you again!"
You'll meet without fail on the Midnight Mail
 The Cat of the Railway Train.

T. S. Eliot
from *Old Possum's Book of Practical Cats*

Flight 524 now boarding at Gate 3.

If you need assistance, please ask your flight attendant for suggestions.

Should you be traveling by car, watch for "Alfa Romeo" and "Ferrari"; they're fast and sometimes difficult to see.

Guarantee your reservation by selecting one of the choices in this chapter. (Cancellations must be made prior to 6 P.M. the day of your pet's arrival.)

Accord	An automobile made by Honda.
Acura	A luxury automobile made by Honda.
Alfa Romeo	An Italian sports car.
Amtrak	American Travel Track; railroad with the most extensive passenger service in the United States; created in 1970.
Audi	German-made automobile.
Bentley	A luxury automobile made by ROLLS ROYCE.
Blazer	A recreational vehicle made by Chevrolet.
BMW (Beemer)	A German-made luxury automobile.
Boeing	An aircraft manufacturer.
Boxcar	A fully enclosed freight car.
Bronco	A recreational vehicle made by FORD.
Bugatti	An Italian sports car.
Buggy	A light, horse-drawn carriage.
Buick	An automobile made by General Motors.
Bus	A large passenger vehicle; also sometimes applied to an old car.
Cadillac	A luxury automobile made by General Motors.

Celica   A sports car made by TOYOTA.

Chevy   Chevrolet: an automobile made by General Motors.

Chrysler   An American automobile/manufacturer.

Corvette   A sports car made by Chevrolet. (See CHEVY.)

DeLorean   An automobile designed and manufactured by John DeLorean in the early 1980s in Belfast, Northern Ireland.

DeSoto   An automobile formerly made by CHRYSLER.

Diesel   Type of internal combustion engine, named for a German engineer.

Dodge   An automobile made by CHRYSLER.

Edsel   An automobile formerly made by FORD.

Ferrari   An Italian sports car.

Ford   An American automobile/manufacturer.

Harley   An American-made motorcycle manufactured by Harley-Davidson, Inc.

Helicopter   An aircraft powered by a rotor.
(Chopper)

Honda   A Japanese automobile/manufacturer.

Jaguar   A British luxury automobile.

Jalopy   Run-down or outdated vehicle (usually a car).

Jeep	An American "general purpose vehicle."
Jet	A type of aircraft engine that propels an aircraft forward by expelling exhaust gases rearward.
Lamborghini	Expensive Italian automobile.
Lexus	Japanese automobile.
Lincoln	American automobile made by FORD.
Lotus	British automobile; no longer manufactured.
Mack	The sturdy, chrome-plated bulldog that stands atop the hood of all Mack trucks.
Mazda	A Japanese automobile/manufacturer.
Mercedes	A German luxury automobile manufactured by Mercedes Benz.
MG	A British sports car.
Mitsubishi	A Japanese automobile/manufacturer.
Nissan	A Japanese automobile/manufacturer.
Peugeot	A French automobile/manufacturer.
Piper	An American aircraft.
Porsche	A German sports car.
Prelude	An automobile made by HONDA.

Rambler	An automobile manufactured in the United States; it is no longer in production.
Regal	An automobile made by BUICK.
Rolls Royce	A British luxury automobile/manufacturer.
Saturn	Four-cylinder Pontiac automobile.
Schooner	A sailing vessel with two or more masts.
Seville	A luxury automobile made by CADILLAC.
Steamer	An early, steam-powered automobile.
Sterling	A British automobile/manufacturer.
Subaru	A Japanese automobile/manufacturer.
Suzuki	A Japanese automobile/manufacturer.
T-Bird	Thunderbird: automobile made by FORD.
Toyota	A Japanese automobile/manufacturer.
Triumph	A British sports car.
Volkswagen	A German automobile/manufacturer.
Volvo	Swedish automobile.
Yamaha	A Japanese motorcycle/manufacturer.

CHAPTER 18

Nature and Science

Nature gives to every time and season some beauties of its own; and from morning to night, as from cradle to the grave, is but a succession of changes so gentle and easy that we can scarcely mark their progress.

Charles Dickens

Take a look at the world of possibilities here. You very well may have a "Gamma" or a "Tiger Lily" just waiting to have the proper title bestowed upon him or her.

Nature and Science

A. C.
Acacia
Acorn
Agate
Alfalfa
Amino
Android
Anion
Anode
Ape
Apollo
Argon
Ariel
Ash
Ashes
Aspen
Aster
Asteroid
Astro
Aurora
Autumn
Axis
Azalea
Badger
Bear
Beaver

Beetle
Begonia
Bengal
Beta
Blizzard
Blossom
Bluebonnet
Boa
Bobcat
Buck
Buckeye
Buckwheat
Buffalo
Bull
Bunny
Buttercup
Butterfly
Byte
Cactus
Calf
Canis Major
Caracal
Carnation
Cat
Catfish
Cathode

Cation
Cheetah
Chick
Cloud
Cobra
Columbine
Comet
Coot
Coral
Corona
Cosmos
Cotton
Coyote
Crab
Cricket
Cub
Cyclone
Cypress
D. C.
Daffodil
Daisy
Dandelion
Delta
Diamond
Dog
Dove

Dynamite
Eagle
Earth
Echo
Eclipse
Equinox
Evening
Feather
Felis
Fern
Fish
Fission
Flint
Flower
Fox
Foxfire
Foxtail
Foxy
Frog
Fungus
Galaxy
Gamma
Garden
'Gator
Goat
Goose

Grizzly	Leopard	Neon	R.E.M.
Halley's Comet	Lightning	Neptune	Rabbit
Halo	Lilac	Newt	Radar
Hawk	Lily	Nocturne	Radon
Hog	Lion	Nova	Rainbow
Holly	Lizard	Nugget	Rose
Honey Bee	Llama	Nuke	Rosebud
Honeysuckle	Lotus	Ocelot	Ruby
Hormone	Lunar	Oleander	Sage
Horse	Lynx	Onyx	Sagebrush
Iguana	Magneto	Orbit	Sassafras
Iris	Magnolia	Orchid	Saturn
Ivy	Marigold	Ozone	Seismis
Jade	Mars	Panda	Serval
Jaguar	Meerkat	Pansy	Shark
Jaguarundi	Megabyte	Panther	Sierra
Jasmine	Mercury	Parasite	Sigma
June Bug	Micro	Petunia	Silver
Jupiter	Micron	Pig	Skunk
Kaffir	Mink	Pigeon	Sky
Kingfish	Mirage	Piranha	Snake
Krypton	Monkey	Pluto	Snapdragon
Larkspur	Moon	Polar	Solar
Laser	Morning Glory	Poppy	Spider
Lava	Mule	Primrose	Squirrel
Leech	Nebula	Puma	Star

Nature and Science

Steroids ("Roids")

Storm

Sun

Sunset

Sunshine

Sunspot

Supernova

Thor (rocket)

Thunder

Tiger

Tiger Lily

Toad

Topaz

Tornado

Tree

Tropical

Tulip

Tumbleweed

Turbo

Turkey

Turtle

Twilight

Uranus

Ursa Minor

Venus

Weasel

Weed

Whale

Wildcat

Willow

Wolf

Worm

Zebra

Zinnia

"Lizard"

"Donut"

CHAPTER 19

Foods

. . . eat, that thou mayest have strength, when thou goest on thy way.

I *Samuel* 28:22

In every veterinarian's files, you will find many pets named after a variety of foods: from "Bagel" and "Biscuit" to "Taffy" and "Truffle." For a perfect pet praenomen, take a look at this sampling of culinary delights.

Foods

Anchovy

Angel Food

Apple

Asparagus

Avocado

Baby Ruth (a brand of candy bar)

Bagel

Banana

Basil

Beef

Berry

Biscuit

Blackberry

Blueberry

Bosco (a brand of chocolate syrup)

Brie (a cheese)

Bromley (a type of apple)

Brownie

Bubble Gum

Butter

Buttercup

Butterfingers (a brand of chocolate candy bar)

Buttermilk

Caramel

Carrot

Cashew

Casserole

Caviar

Chalupa (a type of Mexican food consisting of a flat fried TORTILLA topped with refried beans and cheese)

Cheddar

Cheerio (a brand of breakfast cereal)

Cheesecake

Cheeto (a brand of cheese-flavored corn puff)

Cherry

Chestnut

Chicken

Chili

Chip(s)

Chiquita (a brand of bananas)

Chocolate

Chocolate Chip

Chung King (a brand of Chinese food)

Cinnamon

Cinnamon Muffin

Clove

Cocoa

Coconut

Coffee

Cookie

Crackerjack

Crackers

Crepe (a thin pancake)

Crisco (a brand of shortening)

Croissant

Crouton

Cupcake

Curry (a mixture of spices used in Indian cooking)

Custard

Divinity (Fudge)

Donut

Dorito (a brand of corn chip)

Egg Roll

Eggplant

Enchilada (a type of Mexican food consisting of a TORTILLA filled with meat or cheese)

Escargot (a French delicacy of snails prepared in butter, parsley, and garlic)

Fajita (a type of Mexican food consisting of strips of barbequed meat, usually beef or chicken served with TORTILLAS)

Frankfurter

French Fry

Frito (a brand of corn chip)

Fudge

Ginger

Ginger Snap

Ginseng

Gravy

Grits

Guacamole (mashed and seasoned avacado)

Gum Drop

Gummi Bear (a brand of candy)

Häagen Dazs (a brand of ice cream)

Hershey (a brand of chocolate)

Honey

Hot Dog

Jalapeno (a type of hot pepper)

Jambalaya (a Cajun dish)

Java

Jello

Jelly

Jelly Bean

Jerky (a dried beef snack)

Kibble (a type of dry dog food)

Kiwi

Kuchen (a German coffee cake with a short-bread crust)

Kumquat (a type of citrus fruit)

Lemon

Lemon Drop

Licorice

Lime

Linguini

Lollipop

Macaroni

Mango

Marshmallow

Meatball

Meringue (stiffly beaten egg whites and sugar used as a dessert topping)

Molasses

Muffin

Mushroom

Mustard

Nacho (a type of Mexican food consisting of a CHIP topped with refried beans, cheese and/or jalapeño peppers)

Noodle

Nutmeg

O. J. (orange juice)

Oatmeal

Olive

Onion

Orange

Oreo (a brand of cookie)

Pancake

Paprika

Peaches

Peanut(s)

Pepper

Pepper Shaker

Peppermint

Perugina (dark brown chocolate)

Phyllo (paper-thin sheets of pastry used in the preparation of Greek desserts and appetizers)

Pickles	Relish
Pinto	Rhubarb
Pistachio	Ribeye
Pizza	Ritz (a brand of cracker)
Popsicle	Sage
Popcorn	Salt
Pork Chop	Sassafras (a type of tea)
Potato	Sauce
Pretzel	Sausage
Pringle	Schnitzel
Pudding	Sesame
Pumpernickel	Shortcake
Pumpkin	Shrimp
Quiche	Sirloin
Raisin	Skippy (a brand of peanut butter)
Raisin Bran	Smuckers (a brand of jams and jellies)
Raspberry	Snickers (a brand of candy bar)

Foods

Souffle

Soup

Spaghetti

Spearmint

Spice

Spud (Potato)

Squash

Strawberry

Strudel

Sugar

Sundae

Sushi (a type of Japanese food consisting of raw fish and seasoned rice)

Syrup

T-Bone

Tabasco (a brand of hot sauce)

Taco (a type of Mexican food consisting of a folded TORTILLA filled with meat, cheese and spices)

Taffy

Tamale (a type of Mexican food consisting of minced meat and spices rolled in a corn dough and cooked in a wrapping of a corn husk)

Tangerine

Tapioca Pudding

Tater (potato)

Tenderloin

Tomato

Tootsie Roll

Tortilla (a type of Mexican food consisting of a thin baked circular piece of dough, the main ingredient being corn or flour)

Truffle

Turnip

Twinkie (a brand of snack cake)

Vichyssoise

Waffle

Weiner

Wheatie(s) (a brand of breakfast cereal)

Wishbone

Ziplock (a brand of food storage bags)

"Brandy"

CHAPTER 20

Liquors and Drinks

Let your boat of life be light, packed with only what you
need—a homely home and simple pleasures, one or two
*   nds, worth the name, someone to love you, a cat, a dog,*
*   l a pipe or two, enough to eat and enough to drink; for*
*   ·st is a dangerous thing.*

Jerome Klapka Jerome
from *Three Men in a Boat*

lly up to the bar.
ndoubtedly some of the following names were selected after the pet
rs did so. (Not all the drinks listed are alcoholic).
leers to you!

Liquors and Drinks

Amaretto	Almond LIQUEUR.
Amstel	A brand of beer.
Asahi	A brand of Japanese beer.
Bahama Mama	A cocktail.
Bartles (Bartles and Jaymes)	A brand of wine cooler.
Beaujolais	A type of red wine.
Beaulieu	A California winery.
Beck's	A brand of German beer.
Big Red	A brand of soft drink.
Bordeaux	A type of red wine.
Bourbon	A liquor distilled from a mash of corn, rye, and malted barley.
Brandy	A liquor distilled from fermented grapes or other fruit.
Budweiser	A brand of American beer.
Cabernet (Sauvignon)	A type of red wine.
Canadian Club (C. C.)	A brand of Canadian WHISKEY.

Cappucino   A drink made with strong coffee and hot milk.

Celis   A brand of beer.

Chablis   A type of white wine.

Champagne   An effervescent wine.

Chardonnay   A type of white wine.

Chianti   An Italian red wine.

Chivas (Regal) A brand of Scotch WHISKEY.

Claret   A type of red wine.

Coca-Cola (Coke) A brand of soft drink.

Cocoa   A beverage made from the defatted portion of the cocoa bean.

Coffee   A beverage made from roasted and ground coffee beans.

Cognac   A type of French BRANDY.

Coors   An American beer.

Corona   A brand of Mexican beer.

Courvoisier   A brand of French COGNAC.

Cuervo   A brand of Mexican TEQUILA.

Liquors and Drinks

Daiquiri	A frozen or iced drink made with fruit juice, sugar, and rum.
Dewars	A brand of Scotch WHISKEY.
Dixie	A brand of American beer.
Dos Equis	A brand of Mexican beer.
Dr. Pepper	A brand of soft drink.
Foster's	A brand of beer.
Gin	A liquor flavored with juniper berries.
Glen Ellen	A brand of wine.
Grolsch	A brand of Dutch beer.
Harvey Wallbanger	A cocktail.
Heineken	A brand of Dutch beer.
Hurricane	A cocktail.
Jack Daniels	A brand of Tennesee WHISKEY.
Jax	A brand of American beer
Jaymes (Bartles and Jaymes)	A brand of wine cooler.
Jigger(s)	A measure used in making mixed drinks (usually 1½ ounces).

Kahlúa	A brand of Mexican coffee liqueur.
Kamikaze	A cocktail.
Killian('s)	A brand of American beer.
Kirin	A brand of Japanese beer.
Lemonade	A beverage made with lemon juice, sugar, and water.
Liqueur	A sweetened, flavored liquor.
Mai Tai	A cocktail.
Margarita	A cocktail.
Martini	A cocktail.
Merlot	A type of red wine.
Miller	A brand of American beer.
Mint Julep	A cocktail.
Mocha	A rich Arabian coffee; a drink made by mixing coffee with chocolate.
Molson	A brand of Canadian beer.
Moosehead	A brand of Canadian beer.
Moretti	A brand of Italian beer.

Liquors and Drinks

Mr. Pibb	A brand of soft drink.
Napa	A valley in California where grapes are grown to make wine.
Nehi	A brand of soft drink.
Old Milwaukee	A brand of American beer.
Pabst (Blue Ribbon)	A brand of American beer.
Pearl	A brand of Texas beer.
Pepe Lopez	A brand of Mexican TEQUILA.
Pepsi	A brand of soft drink.
Peroni	A brand of Italian beer.
R. C. Cola	A brand of soft drink.
Root Beer	A soft drink.
Sake	A Japanese alcoholic beverage made from rice.
Samuel Adams	A brand of American beer.
Samuel Smith('s)	A brand of British beer.
Sapporo	A brand of Japanese beer.
Schnapps	Various flavored LIQUEURS.

Scotch	A WHISKEY distilled from malted barley.
Seagram's	A brand of American blended WHISKEY.
Sebastiani	A California wine/winery.
Seven Up	A brand of soft drink.
Shasta	A brand of soft drink.
Shiner Bock	A brand of beer.
Singapore Sling	A cocktail.
Slice	A brand of soft drink.
Soda	A flavored soft drink; unflavored carbonated water; a mixture of the latter with ice cream and syrup.
Soda Pop	A flavored soft drink.
Spatlese	A type of German white wine.
Sprite	A brand of soft drink.
Spritzer	A cocktail.
St. Pauli Girl	A brand of German beer.
Stolychnaya (Stoli)	A brand of Russian VODKA.
Stroh's	A brand of American beer.

Liquors and Drinks

Superior	A brand of Mexican beer.
Swizzle	A cocktail.
Tea	A beverage brewed from the leaves of the tea plant.
Tecate	A brand of Mexican beer.

"Schnapps"

Tequila	A liquor distilled from mescal.
Tonic	Anything that refreshes or rejuvenates; a regional carbonated water.
Tucher Weiss	A brand of beer.
Two Fingers	A brand of Mexican TEQUILA.
Verdillac	A French wine
Vodka	A colorless, "neutral" liquor distilled from grain.
Watney's	A brand of British beer.
Whiskey	Any liquor distilled from a grain mash.
Wild Turkey	A brand of Kentucky WHISKEY.
Xing Tao	A brand of Chinese beer.
Zima	A brand of American beer.
Zinfandel	A red, white, or blush wine made from California's Zinfandel grape.

"L.L. Bean"

CHAPTER 21

Fashion and Cosmetics

The world is governed more by appearances than by realities, so that it is fully as necessary to seem to know something as to know it.

Daniel Webster

You don't have to be an ardent devotee of design to consider some of the names in this chapter. Just the right name for your fashionable pet might be close at hand . . . or on your feet!

Fashion and Cosmetics

Aca Joe	A brand of clothing.
Amethyst	A semiprecious stone.
Anaïs Anaïs	A brand of fragrance.
Benetton	A chain of clothing stores.
Blush	A type of cosmetic used to heighten facial color.
Bongo	A brand of clothing.
Bubble Bath	A scented soap used to produce masses of bubbles in bath water.
Calvin Klein	Designer; brand of clothing.
Cambridge	A brand of clothing.
Carolina Herrera	A brand of fragrance named for the designer.
Cashmere	A fine woolen fabric made from the hair of the kashmir goat.
Chanel	Designer; brand of clothing and fragrance.
Chaps	Protective leather leg coverings worn by cowboys. Also a brand of cologne.
Chic	A brand of clothing; highly fashionable.
Chloë	A brand of fragrance.
Christian Dior	Designer; brand of clothing; fragrance and cosmetics.

Claiborne (Liz)	Designer; brand of clothing and fragrance.
Confetti	A brand of clothing.
Cover Girl	A brand of cosmetics.
Diamond	A precious stone.
Drakkar	A brand of cologne.
Elle	A fashion magazine.
Emerald	A precious stone.
Esprit	A brand of clothing.
Finesse	A brand of shampoo/hair products.
Forenza	A brand of clothing.
Genera	A brand of clothing.
Giorgio	A brand of fragrance.
Girbaud	A brand of clothing.
Gitano	A brand of clothing.
Givenchy	Designer; brand of clothing, fragrance, and cosmetics.
GQ	Men's fashion and lifestyle magazine.

Gucci	Designer; brand of clothing, handbags, etc.
Guess	A brand of clothing.
Haggar	A brand of clothing.
Halston	Designer; brand of cologne and fragrance.
Jack & Jill	A brand of clothing.
Jade	A gemstone, usually pale green or white.
Jasmine	A brand of fragrance.
L. L. Bean	A mail-order clothing company and brand of outdoor clothing products.
Laura Ashley	Designer; brand of clothing, linens, and fragrance.
Lee	A brand of sportswear.
Levi	A brand of sportswear.
Lipstick	A type of cosmetic used to heighten lip color.
Maybelline	A brand of cosmetics.
Obsession	A brand of fragrance and cologne.
Onyx	A black gemstone used in jewelry.
Opal	A gemstone.

Opium	A brand of fragrance and cologne.
Oxford	A style of shoe with laces; a type of cotton cloth.
Paco Rabanne	A brand of fragrance.
Paisley	A multicolored pattern of curving shapes used to decorate fabric.
Paloma Picasso	Designer; daughter of artist Pablo Picasso.
Pappagallo	A brand of shoes.
Paris	A brand of fragrance.
Passion	A brand of fragrance.
Pearl	A lustrous concretion formed inside an oyster.
Poison	A brand of fragrance.
Polo	A brand of clothing designed by RALPH LAUREN.
Poncho	(1) A loose fitting piece of clothing worn by some Mexicans. (2) A garment made of plastic or other waterproof material, used as a raincoat.
Powder Puff	A fluffy applicator for face or body powder.
Ralph Lauren	Designer; brand of clothing.
Revlon	A brand of cosmetics.
Rolex	A brand of wristwatch.

Fashion and Cosmetics

Ruby	A precious stone.
Sapphire	A precious stone.
Satin	A lustrous fabric made of silk or rayon.
Seiko	A brand of wristwatch from Japan.
Shalimar	A brand of fragrance.
Soapy	Sudsy.
Spats	Shoe coverings.
Spiegel	A mail-order clothing company
Sterling	Silver that is nearly pure (925 parts silver to 75 parts copper).
Tiara	A crown of jewels.
Tiffany	A fashionable jewelry store in New York City.
Topaz	A semi-precious stone.
Tux	Short for tuxedo—formal attire for a man.
Vanderbilt (Gloria)	Designer; brand of clothing and fragrance.
Velvet	A fabric made of silk, rayon, etc., which has a soft, luxuriant texture.
Vidal Sassoon	Designer; brand of clothing and hair-care products.

Wrangler   A brand of clothing.

Yves Saint Laurent Designer; brand of clothing.

"Moritz" and *"Max"*

CHAPTER **22**

Pairs

So you're having twice as much fun now that you have two little critters, right? You might as well relax and enjoy it by taking a look at these interesting combinations. Perhaps you'll find that very special one-of-a-kind name for your very special two-of-a-kind friends.

Pairs

Abbott & Costello (See Chapter 11)

Adam & Eve (See Chapter 7)

Amos & Andy (See Chapter 11)

Anion & Cation (See Chapter 18)

Ann & Dan (See Chapter 10)

Anode & Cathode (See Chapter 18)

Antony & Cleopatra

Apples & Oranges

Aurora & Boring Alice (See Chapter 10)

Back & Forth

Barney & Fred (See Chapter 14)

Barnum & Bailey (See Chapter 5)

Baron & Baroness

Bartles & Jaymes (See Chapter 20)

Baucis & Philemon (See Chapter 6)

Bert & Ernie (See Chapter 11)

Betty & Wilma (See Chapter 14)

Big & Bad

Biton & Cleobis (See Chapter 6)

Black & White

Bogey & Bacall (See Chapter 11)

Bonnie & Clyde

Briggs & Stratton (a type of engine)

Cagney & Lacey

Cain & Abel (See Chapter 7)

Calvin & Hobbes (See Chapter 14)

Carlos & Charlie (a restaurant in Mexico)

Castor & Pollux (See Chapter 6)

Chainsaw & Sawdust

Cheech & Chong (comedians)

Count & Countess

Cupid & Psyche (See Chapter 6)

Czar & Czarina

David & Goliath (See Chapter 7)

Ding & Ling

Down & Out

Dr. Jekyll & Mr. Hyde

Dude & Dudette

Duke & Duchess

East & West

Elvis & Priscilla

Emperor & Empress

Felix & Oscar (See Chapter 11)

Ferdinand & Isabella (See Chapter 5)

First & Ten

Foot Loose & Fancy Free

Frank and Stein

Fred & Ethel (See Chapter 11)

George & Gracie (See Chapter 11)

Get Off the Rug & You Too

Glimmer & Twynkle

Groucho & Harpo (See Chapter 15)

Happy & Sad

Harley & Davidson

Hera & Zeus (See Chapter 6)

Hero & Leander (See Chapter 6)

Him & Her (See Chapter 5)

Hollywood & Vine

Hoot & Holler

Hunkie & Dorie

Hunnies & Funnies

Itsy & Bitsy

King & Queen

Kut & Kutta (See Chapter 9)

Pairs

Lady & Tramp (See Chapter 11)

Laurel & Hardy (See Chapter 11)

Laverne & Shirley (See Chapter 11)

Licker & Whiner

Lord & Lady

Love 'Em & Leave 'Em

Lucy & Ricky (See Chapter 11)

Mason & Dixon

Max & Moritz (See Chapter 10)

Mickey & Minnie (See Chapter 14)

Mutt & Jeff (See Chapter 14)

Napoleon & Josephine (See Chapter 5)

Nieman & Marcus (See Chapter 12)

Nip & Tuck

North & South

Now & Then

Null & Void

Orpheus & Eurydice (See Chapter 6)

Ozzie & Harriet (See Chapter 11)

Patience & Fortitude (See Chapter 10)

Patriarch & Matriarch

Pete & Repeat

Ping & Pong

Porgy & Bess

Prince & Princess

Prose & Kahn

Pyramus & Thisbe (See Chapter 6)

Ralph & Alice (See Chapter 11)

Regis & Kathie Lee (See Chapter 11)

Ren & Stimpy (See Chapter14)

Romeo & Juliet (See Chapter 10)

Rough & Ready

Ruff & Tuff

Salt & Pepper

Samson & Delilah (See Chapter 7)

Scarlett & Rhett (See Chapter 11)

Simon & Garfunkel

Simon & Schuster (See Chapter 10)

Sonny & Cher (See Chapter 15)

Stanley & Livingstone (See Chapter 5)

Sugar & Spice

Taco & Chalada (See Chapter 19)

Teeter & Totter

Tick & Tock

Tom & Jerry (See Chapter 14)

Topsy & Turvy

Venus & Adonis (See Chapter 10)

Waylon & Willy

When & If

Wilbur & Charlotte (See Chapter 10)

Wilbur & Orville (See Chapter 5)

Woofer & Tweeter (See Chapter 15)

"Good, Bad & Ugly"

CHAPTER 23

Trios

Love the earth and sun and the animals, despise riches, . . .
have patience and indulgence toward the people, . . . dismiss
whatever insults your soul, and your very flesh shall be a
great poem.

Walt Whitman

Here's a sampling of the many possibilities for owners of three pets.
For additional ideas, consider the topics and names in Chapters 1–21; staying within a given category for all three names makes a more interesting combination.

One word of caution: Names that rhyme may sound confusing to animals. However, if they already seem confused, try Larry, Moe, and Curly.

Trios

Blood, Sweat & Tears (See Chapter 15)

Flopsy, Mopsy & Cottontail (See Chapter 10)

Good, Bad & Ugly

Hey You, Who Me, Yeah You

Hickory, Dickory & Dock

Huey, Dewey & Louie (See Chapter 14)

Larry, Moe & Curly (See Chapter 11)

Peter, Paul & Mary

Upstairs, Downstairs & Mezzanine

REGISTERING A NAME WITH THE AMERICAN KENNEL CLUB

If your dog will be registered by the American Kennel Club (AKC), you need to follow the guidelines established by the AKC:

The person who owns the dog and applies to register it has the right to name the dog. On registration applications issued starting in mid-1989 a space is provided for only one name choice. Registration applications issued prior to that time have spaces for two name choices. It is not necessary to indicate a second name choice, but if you do, consider both names carefully. There is always a chance that the second will be approved and, therefore, it should be equally desirable by the owner. A dog's name may not be changed after it is registered.

Name choices are limited to 25 letters.

No Arabic or Roman numerals may be included in name choices, and no written number is permitted at the end of names. AKC reserves the right to assign a Roman numeral. AKC permits thirty-seven dogs of each breed to be assigned the same name, and many common names such as Spot, Snoopy, Lassie, King, etc., are fully allotted. The shorter the name choice the greater the chances that AKC will assign a Roman numeral or that the name may not be accepted at all. The longer and more unique the name chosen, the greater the chance for approval. The easiest way to lengthen a name is to incorporate your surname, for example, "Smith's Spot" instead of Spot.

Remember that the dog's "call name," that is, the name he responds to, does not have to be the same as his registered name. If you name your dog "Spot" and it is not approved, you may continue to call him "Spot," even though his registered name may be different.

Incorrect spelling and grammar are not corrected by AKC. Names are approved as submitted. A change in spelling is considered a change of name and is not allowed.

Do not include:
1. Names of prominent people, living or recently deceased.
2. Words or abbreviations that imply AKC titles (Champ, Winner).
3. The words: Dog, Male, Sire, Bitch, Female, Dam, Kennel.
4. Words that are disparaging or obscene.
5. Roman or Arabic numerals.
6. Breed names alone.*

To obtain applications or more information concerning AKC registration and requirements, write to:

American Kennel Club
51 Madison Avenue
New York, New York 10010

*American Kennel Club, *Dogs, General Information*, (New York: American Kennel Club), pp. 21–22. Used with permission.

Help me make *The Best Pet Name Book Ever* even better!

Just in case I forgot your favorite pet name, please send it to me so I can include it in the next edition of this book.

If there is a story or explanation behind your choice of name, please include that, too.

Send all nominations for the next edition to:

Wayne Bryant Eldridge
c/o Barron's Educational Series, Inc.
250 Wireless Boulevard
Hauppauge, NY 11788